MARIAN APPARITIONS TODAY
Why So Many?

MARIAN APPARITIONS TODAY
Why So Many?

Fr. Edward D. O'Connor, C.S.C.

Queenship

PUBLISHING COMPANY
P.O Box 42028 Santa Barbara, CA 93140-2028
(800)647-9882 Fax: (805) 569-3274

©1996 Queenship Publishing

Library of Congress Number # 96-067811

Published by:
Queenship Publishing
P.O. Box 42028
Santa Barbara, CA 93140-2028
(800)647-9882   Fax: (805) 569-3274

Printed in the United States of America

ISBN: 1-882972-71-6

Contents

Dedication

To the prayer groups of the Notre Dame / South Bend area for whose intercession I am deeply indebted, especially:

The Log Chapel Group
The Medjugorge Group
The Knights of the Imaculata
The Children of Mary
The St. Stephen's Group
The Holy Family Group
The nameless group centered around and animated by the inspiring example of Rudy and Jackie Prikosovich.

Introduction

When I was a small boy, my mother used to warn me about playing in the busy street right in front of our house. One day, without thinking, I ran out into the street to retrieve a ball. Although I was only three years old, I can still remember the frightened driver of the car, who had pulled over, thinking he had hit me, and my neighbor next door who came running. Miraculously, I was not run over because our neighbor's dog pulled me back to safety by the seat of my pants. I had forgotten my mother's warning.

In this book Father O'Connor details many of the warnings that have been given to us by our Heavenly Mother. The Church does not usually judge these messages, although some have received ecclesiastical approbation. But because the messages do call us to conversion, prayer and penance, many of us are brought closer to God and His Blessed Mother. May your reading of this book motivate you to additional prayer and penance for our sinful and suffering humanity.

Most Reverend Donald W. Montrose
Bishop of Stockton
October 12, 1994

Author's Preface

This book has arisen out of talks given on various occasions, not originally intended to come together in one work. The first chapter is based on a presentation given at the National Medjugorje Conference held at the University of Notre Dame, May 12-14, 1989.

The second was composed for a program on the Blessed Virgin organized by Mr. Thomas Eckrich at St. Elizabeth Seton Church in Fort Wayne, October 27, 1994.

The third was addressed to the International Mariological Conference at Huelva, Spain, September 18-27, 1992. In a slightly different form from the present one, it is to be published in the proceedings of that conference.

The fourth was given first at the National Medjugorje Conference at Notre Dame, May 20-22, 1994.

The fifth originated out of some comments offered as background for Dominican Father Frederick Jelly's address, "Norms for judging apparitions and private revelations," at the national conference of the Mariological Society of America at Providence College, May 27 and 28, 1993.

The bibliography was drawn up in conjunction with chapter 3.

For the present edition, all the essays have been modified and adapted in order to fit together coherently.

The cover photograph depicts the "Mystical Rose" of Montechiari, Italy, modeled on the description given by Pierina Gilli to whom Mary is said to have appeared, beginning on December 8, 1947. (Like many other alleged apparitions, these have not been recounted in the present book, because it was simply impossible to make a serious study of so many accounts; the omission does not betoken any positive disbelief on my part.[1]) The statue, carved according to Pierina's description by the sculptor Cajo Perathonner,

---

[1] A detailed account of the apparitions in Montechiari, and of the weeping statue in St. John of God Church, can be found in *Mary the Mystical Rose* by A.M. Weigle, second edition published by Father Raymond Jasinski, Chicago, 1988.

was erected in the parish church of Montechiari by the pastor, Msgr. Abbate Rossi. Since then, many copies have been made and taken to various parts of the world for veneration, and innumerable reports of miracles concerning them have been recounted.

Our cover photograph represents one of these copies, hand-carved in wood, and purchased in 1984 by Mr. Anthony Di Cola of Chicago. He actually procured two copies, one of which he kept in his home, while the other he donated to Father Raymond Jasinski, pastor of St. John of God Church in Chicago. On May 29, 30 and 31 the latter statue, standing in the sanctuary of the church, wept tears. The weeping was witnessed by an estimated 200 people, including two priests, seven Felician sisters who conducted the parish school, the janitor and a policeman (the latter two tasted the tears and found them to be salty, like human tears). The face of the statue also appeared swollen. Our photograph was taken by Father Jasinski.

One of the priests, Msgr. Thad Wincenciak, of the diocese of Chicago, did not believe the weeping was genuine, adding that his faith had no need of that sort of signs. As he and others were visiting the Di Cola home, Mr. Di Cola's statue also began to weep. Other witnesses to the weeping of this second statue were Father Ted Hochstatter of Peoria, Deacon Rafaele di Rosa from Sicily, Fr. John Starace of Brooklyn, together with the latter's father and nephew, and Robert Di Cola, Anthony's son.

After receiving reports about these weeping statues, Cardinal Bernardin, the Archbishop of Chicago, appointed a committee to investigate the matter. One year later, in May of 1985, the committee, headed by Bishop Alfred Abramowicz, reported that "the results of tests, consultation and interviews are such that it is impossible to render a definite judgment as to the nature of the phenomenon. ...we are not able to eliminate the possibility that natural causes might explain the occurrence."[2]

---

[2] From the report presented by Father James Roache, Moderator of the Archdiocesan Curia, to the Presbyteral Senate of the Archdiocese of Chicago at its meeting of September 17, 1985.

I am deeply grateful to Ms. Cheryl Reed for typing the manuscript so expertly and accurately; to Mrs. Patricia Bayliss for helpful stylistic corrections; to Mr. Nicholas Vakkur for composing the chart on p. xx, as well as researching the copyrights to the illustrations; to Fathers Donald Paradis, S.M. and Roger Plante, S.M., whose critique enabled me to make a more impartial report on the "Secret of La Salette"; to Mr. Robert Schaefer of Queenship for agreeing to publish the work; and to both Ms. Reed and Mr. Schaefer for their patience in enduring repeated modifications of the original text.

I am greatly indebted also to Mr. Robert Ringel of the University of Notre Dame for the drawings of the Miraculous Medal, p. 5, and of the front of the Green Scapular, p. 6; to Rev. Martin Lam Nguyen, C.S.C. for the drawing of the reverse side of the Green Scapular, p. 6; and to Mrs. Marge Gloster for the lettering around these images.

I want to thank likewise the following persons for the use of their photographs:

Mother Agnes Therese of the Infant Jesus, O.C.D., prioress of the Monastery of Our Lady of Guadalupe, Ada, MI (St. Simon Stock, p. 70);

Mrs. Patricia Bayliss (Brother David Lopez, p. 39);

The rector of the Sanctuary of Beauraing (the Immaculate Virgin of Beauraing, p. 15);

The Biblliothéque Nationale in Paris (Gregory the Great, p. 45, Jesus appearing to Mary Magdalene, p. 82

R.P. Hervé Bougeard, S.M. rector of the Sanctuary of La Salette (Maximin Melanie and Our Lady of La Salette, p. 10);

Rev. Leonard Boyle, O.P., of the Vatican Library (Fifth Lateran Council, p. 121);

Mr. Louis Ciesielski of South Bend (Medjugorje Conference at the University of Notre Dame, June 2-4, 1995, p. 68);

The Franciscan friars of Marytown (Our Lady of Fatima Friary), Libertyville, IL. (The Annunication, p. 81;

Garabandal Magazine (Garabandal, p. 2, the visionaries, p. 16 Conchita, pp. 18 and 19, and Padre Pio, p. 103;

Father Joseph-Marie Jacq., M.E.P. (Our Lady of Akita weeping, p. 26, photographed by himself);

Mr. Stanley Karminski (Betania Finca, p. 23);

Mr. Sang M. Lee of *Mary's touch by mail* (Julia Kim's bleeding statue, p. 26);

The rector of the Santuario della Madonna delle Lacrime (the weeping Madonna of Syracuse, p. 26);

Marian Communications, Lima Pa. (Maria Esperanza, p. 22

The Marian Helpers, Stockbridge, MA. (Sister Faustina, p. 113);

Sister Mechthild, editor of *Triumph des Herzens*, and Mrs. Betsy War, of Denver, CO (Berthe Petit p. 27);

Dr. Brian Miller of Cleveland (the rosary being held up for blessing, p. 17, the rosary being returned to its owner, p. 17);

Mr. William Reck and the Riehle Foudation (the church of the Blessed Trinity at Hrushiv, p. 24);

Mr. Robert Ringel (the Immaculate Heart, p. 59);

Becky Rhoads of Charleston, IL (Father Gobbi, p. 43);

Rev. Daniel Sharmot, S.M. (Maximin and Melanie, p. 10 and Our Lady of La Salette, p. 10;

Cardinal Jozef Suenens and Sister Marie-Hélène of the Bernardine Cistercian nuns of Notre-Dame de Bon-Secours monastery in Peruwelz, Belgium (the Sorrowful and Immaculate Heart of Mary, p. 29);

Pearl Zaki (the apparition at Zeitun, p. 1).

Scriptural texts are cited from the New American Bible, with the Revised New Testament.

Edward D. O'Connor, C.S.C.
January 28, 1995
Feast of St. Thomas Aquinas

– I –
THE MAJOR MODERN
MARIAN APPARITIONS

Apparitions of the Blessed Virgin and kindred phenomena are being reported more frequently today than ever before in the history of the Church. Besides Medjugorje, which is world-famous, in recent years there have been reports from Italy (Tre Fontane, Sicily, San Damiano, Montechiari), Egypt (Zeitun), Spain (Garabandal, Es-corial), Rwanda (Kibeho), Japan (Akita), Korea (Naju), Canada (Montreal), Syria (Damas-cus), Iraq (Mo-

Actual photograph of Mary as she was seen by thousands of people at Zeitun, Egypt in 1968 and 1969. From Pearl Zaki, *Our Lord's Mother Visits Egypt in 1968 & 1969,* p.30

zul), Ireland (many places), Venezuela, Ecuador, Argentina, Nicaragua, and Ukraine. In addition to these well-established examples, innumerable others are just barely beginning to become known, for example, in Slovakia, Hungary, Taiwan, Vietnam, Puerto Rico, South Africa, Costa Rica, Cameroon, Lithuania, Zaire, the Philippines, France and Peru. In the United States alone, there have been recent reports of such events in Chicago, Phoenix, Texas (Lubbock), Georgia (Conyers), Ohio (Youngstown), Colorado (Denver), Virginia (Lake Ridge), Indiana (Bloomington), and Kentucky (Cold Springs), besides many lesser known ones. Cardinal Ratzinger has declared that, "one of the signs of our times is that the announcements of `Marian apparitions' are multiplying all over the world."[1] And the number of

---

[1] *The Ratzinger Report*, San Francisco (Ignatius Press, 1985), p. 111.

people who claim to have experienced private encounters with Our Lady in their personal lives is countless.

This can be disconcerting. Pastors worry about people who have a thirst for the extraordinary instead of the solid staples of the spiritual life. Theologians are concerned about the danger of replacing the solid teachings of the Gospel with new ideas based on private revelations. Sociologists speculate that the anxiety of our age may be driving people to wishful thinking. Any thinking person is tempted to wonder whether we aren't witnessing a sort of craze, in which people in one place are being excited by those in another. Even those deeply devoted to Mary sometimes feel a certain distress at trying to find place in their lives for devotions to Our Lady under all these titles.

I remember well how this problem arose in my own life. When I was a boy, about the only Marian apparition much talked about was Lourdes. During the Second World War, we began to hear a great deal about Fatima, where Mary had predicted the Second World War. For a period the Church was divided in a pious rivalry between those more devoted to Our Lady of Lourdes, and those attracted to Fatima. Our Lady of Lourdes was definitely more popular, for she was a smiling mother who brought healing to her children. Still, many found themselves more deeply moved by the somber figure of Our Lady of Fatima warning of danger.

Later I spent four years in France doing graduate studies in theology. There I became acquainted with several more apparitions of which I had heard very little previously: Pontmain, Banneux, Beauraing and others. They left me vaguely uncomfortable, not sure what account I ought to make of them in my devotion to Mary.

Garabandal

Back in this country, I was teaching theology at the University of Notre Dame in the 1960's, when a summer school student asked, "Have you heard of Mary's apparitions at Garabandal?" "No," I replied, "and I don't want to hear of them." She persisted in giving me a brief account, which I read without forming any particular opinion about it.

In 1967, having to go to Lisbon for the International Mariological Conference, I took that occasion to investigate Garabandal. I spent a day and a half there, speaking with Father Valentín Marichalar, the pastor, and two of the visionaries (Jacinta and Mari Loli). I visited the village church, "the Pines," and the place of the miraculous host. I saw nothing miraculous or extraordinary; but on the train from Salamanca, assessing my impressions, I realized that I was now convinced of the genuineness of this apparition. At the same time, it began to dawn on me that the purpose of these multiple apparitions was not to turn our prayer life into a burdensome litany of special devotions. Rather, Mary is a concerned mother, trying by every possible means to get her children's attention. It doesn't matter greatly whether Lourdes or Fatima or Knock or Czestochowa is the focal point of their devotion, so long as they heed what she has to say.

Further investigation made it evident that the various apparitions harmonize coherently, even though each one has a distinctive emphasis and coloring. To see this, it helps to look at the modern series of apparitions as a whole, beginning in 1830.[2] Mary had, of

---

[2] There are books giving more detailed accounts of these apparitions. For the earlier ones, from the Miraculous Medal to Garabandal, the most accurate and sensitive report is *The Immaculate Heart of Mary*, by Father Joseph Pelletier, A.A. (Assumption Publications, POG 227, Worcester, MA 01606), unfortunately no longer in print. The more recent apparitions are reported in *The Thunder of Justice*, by Ted and Maureen Flynn and in the review, *Signs of the Times*, edited by the same couple (both available from 109 Executive Dr. Suite D, Sterling VA 20166); also in *The Final Hour*, by Michael Brown (Faith, PO 237, Milford, OH 45150).

Other general surveys (in chronological order): *The Woman Shall Conquer*, by J. Sharkey (Bruce, Milwaukee, 1952). *The Sun Her Mantle*, by John Beevers (Brown and Nolan, Dublin, 1953). *A Woman Clothed With the Sun*, edited by J. Delaney (Doubleday, New York, 1961). *Those Who Saw Her*, by Catherine Odell (Our Sunday Visitor, Huntington, IN, 1986). *Mother of Nations*, by Joan Ashton (The Lamp Press, Basingstoke, Hants England, 1988). *Encountering Mary*, by Sandral Zimdars-Swartz (Avon Books, New York, 1991).

course, appeared many times before that; the earliest recorded instance dates from the third century. But the early apparitions were for the benefit of individual persons or particular localities. At most they resulted in shrines, the more famous of which drew pilgrims from a distance, e.g., Saragossa in Spain, Le Puy in France, Walsingham in England. While no sharp line of discrimination can be drawn, the modern apparitions seem to be characterized by the impact they have on the Church as a whole. Typically, they bring messages addressed to all the faithful.

They fall into two main types. One type is represented by Lourdes, where, against the magnificent background of the

Pyrennees mountains, Mary smiled and opened up a spring of water that has brought healing and encouragement to thousands of people. In the other type, situated in the dull, dry pastureland of Fatima, she was somber and spoke ominously about dangers that threatened. There is no contradiction between these two

Lourdes – The Grotto Lies in the dark area beneath the Basilica

messages. Both come from the heart of a mother, reaching out in love to her children either to comfort or to protect them. A third theme, synthesizing the other two, is that of the Immaculate Heart of Mary, which has gradually become the focus of attention during the last hundred and sixty years.

Beginning, therefore, with the Miraculous Medal apparition in 1830, we will see these three themes continually reappear and inter-

Fatima

mingle: the smiling Mother who encourages her children, the somber Mother who warns of danger, and the Immaculate Heart, the root from which both of these sentiments arise.

In all this, we will stick strictly to what is actually said and done in the apparitions. There are books which attempt to interpret the messages of Our Lady by relating them to world events and to each other and by speculating about the concrete way in which they will be fulfilled. St. John of the Cross warns us against such endeavors. The moment we go beyond what is actually said in a revelation and undertake our own interpretation, we are very liable to err.[3]

The Miraculous Medal (1830)

The first of the great modern Marian apparitions occurred in 1830.[4] Catherine Labouré was a novice with the Sisters of Charity when Mary appeared to her in Paris, asking that a medal be struck with the inscription, **"O Mary conceived without sin, pray for us who have recourse to thee."** The front of the medal was to bear the image of Mary crushing the serpent's head beneath her feet. Rays descend from her hands, representing the graces she bestows. (When asked why no rays fell from some of her fingers, Mary replied that they stood for the graces that are not received because people fail to ask for them.) The back of the medal bears the letter M surmounted by a cross, and beneath it the two hearts, that of Jesus crowned with thorns, and that of Mary, pierced by a sword. (When Sister Catherine asked if there shouldn't be an inscription on the back to balance the one on the front, Mary replied, "The M and those two hearts say enough.")

---

[3] In the case of some prophecies that seem to have been fulfilled already, this will be pointed out; but that is not the same as making guesses about the future.

[4] See *Catherine Labouré and the Modern Apparitions of Our Lady*, by Omer Engelbert (New York, Kennedy, 1959). René Laurentin, *The Life of Catherine Labouré* (Collins, London, 1983).

The medal appeared in 1832, when Paris was in the midst of a plague of cholera, from which 20,000 people died in a single month. So many miraculous healing were reported by those who wore the medal that it quickly came to be nicknamed, "The Miraculous Medal." In one class of thirty girls taught by the sisters, 29 wore the medal; the thirtieth, who did not wear it, was the only one to contract cholera. When she too accepted the medal, she recovered.

This apparition is very similar to that of Lourdes - Mary coming to heal the sick. But it has another aspect not so well known. Mary once said to Sister Catherine, with a sad look on her face, **"Evil times are coming. France is going to suffer much. The throne will be overturned and the whole world will be upset by evils of every sort."** She added that the clergy were going to suffer, the Archbishop would be stripped of his robes, and another bishop, fleeing persecution, would be sheltered by the Vincentian Fathers. Finally she insisted, **"The entire world will be in distress."** As she said these things, tears flowed from her eyes, and she could hardly continue speaking.

Nine days later, a revolution broke out quite unexpectedly in France, forcing King Charles X to abdicate. Its fierce anti-clericalism obliged the Archbishop of Paris to flee the city while

The Revolution of 1830

another bishop sought shelter with the Vincentians, as Catherine had predicted. It was largely because of these predictions that the Archbishop was persuaded to allow the medal to be printed.

This apparition can be regarded as the root of all the modern Marian apparitions. It touched off the great Marian movement of modern times, and powerfully fostered requests for the definition of the Dogma of the Immaculate Conception, which took place in 1854. Finally it contained in germ the messages of the other apparitions that were to follow. The smiling Madonna who brings health is paramount; but the sad-faced mother warning of danger is also present. While the Immaculate Heart is not mentioned in so many words, the heart of Mary is represented in close relationship with the heart of Jesus, along with a reference to the Immaculate Conception.

The Green Scapular (1840)

Ten years later, Mary appeared to another French nun named Sister Justine. She was a Sister of Charity, like Catherine Labouré; but whereas Catherine was a simple peasant assigned to look after the chicken coop, Justine was a very intelligent and gifted woman, holding some of the most important positions in her community.

Mary appeared to Sister Justine holding her heart in her hands, with flames rising from it. After repeating this several times, she came one day carrying a green scapular. The front bore an image of Mary in the posture in which she had appeared. On the reverse was the heart of Mary, pierced with a sword, surmounted by flames of fire, and encircled by the invocation, **"Immaculate heart of Mary**

pray for us now and at the hour of our death." Here the invocation of Mary's Immaculate Heart is made explicit. This scapular was intended especially to obtain the conversion of unbelievers.

Note that neither the Green Scapular nor the Miraculous Medal as they are currently in use correspond exactly to those requested by Mary. On the Miraculous Medal, the stars that encircled Mary's head in the vision were put on the reverse side by the printer. In the case of the Green Scapular, Father Aladel deleted the rays which were supposed to fall from Mary's hands, as they do in the Miraculous Medal.[5]

It is curious that, six years later (in 1845), a third French Sister of Charity, Apolline Andriveau, received from the hands of Jesus the "Scapular of the Passion of our Lord and of the Sacred Hearts of Jesus and Mary." This was intended to make people meditate more on the Passion of Our Lord, which was represented on one panel. The other panel bore the hearts of Jesus and Mary, as they appear on the Miraculous Medal.

Our Lady of Victories (1836)

Meanwhile attention had been drawn to the Heart of Mary at a famous Church in Paris dedicated to Our Lady of Victories. The church had been desecrated during the French Revolution and later turned into a stock exchange. Eventually it was restored as a Church and Father Des Genettes was appointed its pastor in 1832 (the year of the Miraculous Medal). On the new pastor's first Sunday there, only four parishioners showed up for Mass. He struggled for years to bring the people back, with very meagre results. Throughout all of 1835, only 720 communions were received: an average of less than 14 a week.

One day in 1836, as Father Des Genettes was offering Mass, he was so concerned about how God would judge him that it interfered with his prayer. He prayed to be rid of this distraction so he could consecrate the Eucharist worthily, when he distinctly heard the words, **"Consecrate your parish to the very Holy and Immaculate Heart of Mary."** At the same moment, he was filled with peace and was

---

[5] See the pamphlet, *The Green Scapular*, by Marie Edouard Mott, C.M. St. Joseph's College, Emmitsburg, Md., 1942) and ch. 3 of *The Immaculate Heart of Mary* by Joseph Pelletier, A.A. (Assumption Publications, Worcester, MA, 1976).

able to continue the Mass with recollection and devotion.

After Mass, pondering the matter, he began to think he had imagined it all. But just as he was about to leave the Church, he again heard distinctly the same words, **"Consecrate your parish to the very Holy and Immaculate Heart of Mary."** Now he knew that it had not been his imagination. With great hesitation, he drew up plans for a confraternity in honor of Mary. The following Sunday, in a trembling voice, he announced devotions to be held that evening for the conversion of sinners through the intercession of Mary's Immaculate Heart.

Father Des Genettes

There were only ten men in the congregation that morning. Father Des Genettes was startled when two of them who seldom went to the sacraments came into the sacristy to go to confession. He was even more amazed that evening, when four or five hundred people attended the special services. Still he asked God for a sign, and the sign he requested was the conversion of a certain Mr. Joly.

This eighty year old man had been anti-clerical all his life. Now close to death, he had rejected every effort of the pastor to get him to the sacraments. Father Des Genettes went and tried again. The housekeeper did not want to let him in, but finally he got past her and into the old man's room. After a brief greeting, Mr. Joly asked for a blessing, which startled Father Des Genettes and moved him deeply. The man declared, "Father, I can't see you, yet I feel your presence. Since you came in, I have felt a peace, calm, and inner happiness I have never known before."

From then on, Father Des Genettes preached devotion to Mary's Immaculate Heart with all his energy. The following year, he had 8,550 communions, over ten times as many as the previous year. After one more year, it had risen above 12,000, while nearly 8,000 people enrolled in his Confraternity.[6]

---

[6] See chapter 2 of *The Immaculate Heart of Mary* by Joseph Pelletier, A.A.

La Salette (1846)

Ten years later, Mary appeared again in France, this time to two shepherd children.[7] High up in the foothills of the French Alps, Melanie and Maximin were watching their families' cattle. After dozing off to sleep, they awakened to see a great globe of light resting on the ground where they had been playing a little while before. It opened up to reveal the figure of a woman seated with her head in her hands. She stood up and called them closer. She was beautiful and they immediately felt a great love for her. With tears flowing from her eyes, she said:

If my people do not submit willingly, I shall be forced to allow the arm of my Son to come down upon them. How long a time have I grieved because of you! I have had to pray unceasingly lest my Son abandon you. You can never understand how much sorrow I have known.

She went on to complain about the villagers' poor religious practice, which was why the potato crop had been spoiled the year before. Mary warned that during the coming year, not only potatoes, but wheat, nuts and grapes would rot, causing a famine. This actually came to pass; the

---

[7] See *Light on the Mountain. The Story of La Salette*, by John S. Kennedy (New York, Doubleday, 1956). *The Holy Mountain of La Salette*, by W. B. Ullathorne (La Salette Press, Altamont, N.Y. 1942). *The Abbé Jots it Down*, by Abbé Lagier (La Salette Press, Altamont, N.Y., 1946).

next year, 1847, terrible food shortages in France led to angry popular uprisings in various places. These same conditions produced the great potato famine in Ireland, which drove thousands of our ancestors to America.

Mary also confided a secret to each of the visionaries. These were written down and sent to the Pope in 1851, but the documents seem to have been lost. In 1879, Melanie published her "secret," which fills more than ten pages of a printed pamphlet. The contents are obscure and confused: references to contemporary affairs, predictions of the near future, and allusions to apocalyptic events of the end times are mingled pele-mele. The Pope is warned that he will have much to suffer, and that he is not to leave the Vatican after 1859. (In 1860 Italy began the annexation of the Papal States that left the pope a "prisoner of the Vatican" for the next hundred years.) The "secret" also declares that Satan and many other demons would be let out of hell in 1864, with baleful consequences, especially for priestly and religious vocations. A future world war, a crisis in the Church, the birth of an Antichrist who will reign out of Rome, and the final victory of the archangel Michael are all announced.

Does this document, published in 1879, faithfully represent the secret confided to Melanie in 1846? Many, especially among the Missionaries of La Salette (a community formed in 1852 to care for the shrine), believe that, during the years following the apparition, this backward peasant girl came under the influence of "troubled and sick persons" who were themselves obsessed with popular prophecies and pseudo-apocalyptic views. Absorbing these into her own thoughts, she eventually amalgamated them into the secret confided to her by Our Lady. Others regard Melanie as an authentic mystic, persecuted by people who did not understand her, and disappointed with the failure of the La Salette missionaries to conform to the rule imparted to her by the Blessed Mother. Both interpretations can find support in the troubled career of this socially awkward girl. After a time in a boarding school for which she was ill prepared, she was welcomed as a candidate by the Sisters of Providence, but an unsympathetic bishop would not allow her to be professed. Several attempts at convent life elsewhere all failed, and her last seventeen years were spent in lonely exile at Castellamare, Italy, where the bishop had great veneration for her.

This is not the place to attempt to resolve this debate; for us, the "secret of La Salette" can stand as a prime example of the difficulty of discernment in such matters.

Lourdes (1858)

Twelve years later Mary appeared to Bernadette at Lourdes.[8] Today

this is the most famous of all the Marian apparitions. Everyone has heard how little Bernadette, gathering firewood for her poor parents, saw the beautiful woman in the grotto, smiling. The woman directed Bernadette to drink from a spring that had barely begun to flow;

The Grotto in 1858

since then thousands of people have received healing from its waters. When asked her name, the woman folded her hands, raised her eyes to heaven, and answered, "I am the Immaculate Conception." This was only four years after the dogma had been defined in Rome, and came as a heavenly confirmation of the Pope's action.

We have already noted that Lourdes is the archetype of the tender, smiling Madonna; but it has another aspect that is not so well known. The first thing Mary said to Bernadette was, **"Do penance. Pray to God for the conversion of sinners."** She told Bernadette to kiss the ground and to eat the leaves of a bitter herb as an act of penance. She taught her how to pray the rosary. In other words,

---

[8] See *Bernadette of Lourdes. A Life Based on Authentic Documents*, by Rene Laurentin (Minneapolis, Winston, 1979).

Bernadette praying

even at Lourdes Mary came, not only to offer encouragement and heal the sick, but also to call for penance, prayer and conversion. And she told Bernadette, **"I do not promise you happiness in this world."**

After Lourdes, there is a long interval of 63 years without any major apparitions. There were indeed a few minor ones: In 1871 at Pontmain in France, and in 1876 at Pellevoisin in Belgium, Mary appeared, beseeching, **"If people would only pray."** In 1879 Mary and the Holy Family were seen as figures standing by the wall of the parish church in Knock, Ireland; but no message was given (Mary's silent presence was sufficient message for the suffering people of Ireland!)

Fatima (1917)

The next great apparition took place at Fatima in Portugal. During the summer of 1917, in the midst of the First World War, Mary appeared six times to three children, Lucia, Francisco and Jacinta.[9] Each time she insisted on the need to do penance and make sacrifices for the conversion of sinners.

---

[9] The literature on Fatima is enormous, but mostly in foreign languages. A brief account written by Sister Lucia herself is to be had in *Fatima in Lucia's Own Words* (Postulation Center, Fatima, Portugal). Two standard English accounts, somewhat outdated, however, are: *Fatima, the Great Sign* by Francis Johnston (1980; recently republished by Tan Books, Rockford, IL) and *Our Lady of Fatima* by William Thomas Walsh (Doubleday, 1954). More authoritative is *Fatima from the Beginning*, by Joao de Marchi, I.M.C. (fifth ed. Fatima, Portugal, 1985). The most complete and recent discussion in English, very tendentious, however, is *The Whole Truth about Fatima* by Michel de la Sainte Trinité (Immaculate Heart Publications, Box 1028 Buffalo NY 14205, 1989). *Soul* magazine (The Blue Army of Our Lady of Fatima, Asbury, N.J. 08802) provides on-going information about events connected with the shrine.

In the apparition of July 13, the children were given a frightening vision of hell. Mary said to them, **"You have seen hell, where**

The Visionaries

the souls of sinners go. It is to save them that God wants to establish in the world devotion to my Immaculate Heart. If you do what I tell you, many souls will be saved and there will be peace."

This apparition has probably been the most powerful factor of all in fostering devotion to the Immaculate Heart. But Mary also gave two warnings. First, that if men did not refrain from offending God, another and more terrible war would begin under Pius XI. In fact, it was toward the end of his papacy that the Second World War had its beginnings.

Secondly, Mary warned, **"If my wishes are fulfilled, Russia will be converted and there will be peace. If not, then Russia will spread her errors throughout the world, bringing new wars and persecution of the church. The good will be martyred and the Holy Father will have much to suffer. Certain nations will be annihilated."**

Our Lady of Fatima

She added, however, the reassurance, **"In the end, my Immaculate Heart will triumph. The Holy Father will consecrate Russia to me and she will be converted, and the world will enjoy a period of peace."**

At the time Mary said this, Russia was in a state of total collapse. Its army was being routed by the Germans. The Tsar had been overthrown, and the provisional government of Kerensky was proving impotent. The Marxists were fomenting revolution,

The failed Bolshevic Revolution St. Petersburg, Russia. July 1917

but even they were divided into warring factions - the red Bolsheviks and the white Menscheviks, and it was not yet clear which
would prevail. At that moment, Russia was a threat to no one but
the Russians themselves.

Less than one month later, the Bolsheviks, under the leadership of Lenin, proclaimed the "dictator-
ship of the proletariat." Thus began the
tyranny of atheistic communism, which
engulfed the eastern half of the globe
over the next seventy years, and seems
to be collapsing in our own day. In 1984,
the Holy Father consecrated Russia,
along with the entire world, to the Immaculate Heart of Mary. The very next
year, Gorbachev became head of the
Soviet government and began to set in
motion the policies of *glasnost* and
perestroika that led inexorably to the
ruin of the Communist party, the disso-
lution of the Soviet Union and the beginnings of religious liberty in Russia.

Lenin

Beauraing and Banneux (1932-1933)

In 1932, Mary appeared at Beauraing in
Belgium, her heart visible, golden in
color and emitting rays of light. A year
later, she appeared in another Belgian
town of Banneux. On both occasions, she
repeated over and over, **"Pray, Pray very
much."**

The apparitions discussed thus far
have either been approved by the Church,
or are at least so commonly accepted that
their authenticity is no longer in question.
Now we turn to some more recent ones,
on most of which the Church has not yet
made any judgment.

Beauraing

Garabandal (1961-1965)

In the tiny mountain village of Garabandal in northern Spain, Mary is said to have appeared daily, and sometimes many times a day, to

The four visionaries in ecstasy

four eleven year old girls for a period of 15 months beginning in 1961.[10] Often she led them in ecstasy through the lanes of the village. Looking up into the air at her, without a glance at the ground, they followed her without ever stumbling. They climbed a rocky path up the mountainside in the same way, and sometimes even came down it walking backwards, without ever losing their step. Often they moved so fast that others could not keep up with them, but they were never out of breath. At other times, one would pick another up and hold her in the air to kiss the Blessed Mother, and they would do this as effortlessly as if they had no weight. But a strong young workman of the village told me that once when one of the girls was in ecstasy, he tried to pick her up to protect her from the crush of people, but found her so heavy he could hardly lift her. (It is not uncommon for an unnaturally great weight to be associated with ecstasy.)

Jacinta

The girls began giving Mary rosaries, medals and the like for her to kiss; then returned them to the owner. They always gave

---

[10] See *Our Lady Comes to Garabandal* by Joseph Pelletier, A.A. (Assumption Publication, 500 Salisbury St., Worcester, MA 01609). *The Apparitions of Garabandal*, by F. Sanchez-Ventura y Pascual (San Miguel, Detroit, 1966). *Star on the Mountain*, by M. Laffineur and M. T. Le Pelletier (Our Lady of Mt. Carmel of Garabandal, Newtonville N.Y. 1968). *Miracle at Garabandal* by H. Daley (Ward River Press, Dublin, 1985). *Garabandal, the Village Speaks*, by H. Pérez (The Workers of Our Lady of Mt. Carmel, Lindenhurst, N.Y., 1981). On-going information about Garabandal can be obtained from the quarterly magazine, *Garabandal* (P.O.B. 606, Lindenhurst, N.Y. 11757).

Mari-Loli holding rosaries for Mary to bless them.

them to the right person, often without looking at the person. Even when people began playing tricks on them by changing positions in the crowd, the girls were not fooled. Once thirty women came with their rosaries all in one sack. When they arrived at Garabandal, the rosaries were so entangled with one another the women gave up an attempt to separate them, and handed them to the girls in one big mass. After they had been kissed by Mary, one of the girls pulled them out effortlessly, one by one, and gave each to its rightful owner.

Mary spoke and prayed, laughed, sang and even played with the girls in a motherly fashion that scandalized some people, who would have expected the Mother of God to be more solemn. Most of her conversations did not treat of sublime matters, but of the little everyday events in the girls' lives - work in the fields and even their suntan.

On October 18, 1961, however, Mary gave a very solemn message:

Blessed rosary being returned to its owner

> We must do much penance and make many sacrifices. We must often visit the Blessed Sacrament. But, above all, we must be very good for, if we are not, we will be punished. The cup is already filling up and if we do not amend our lives there will come a great chastisement.

Many people, expecting some spectacular announcement, felt disillusioned by this apparently banal message and quit going to Garabandal. But if studied carefully, the message can be seen to embrace the whole Christian life in language suited to children.

Three years later (June 18, 1964), through Conchita alone, Mary gave a second message, much more somber:

*Conchita at the time
of the apparitions*

Since my message of October 18 has not been made known to the world and has not been fulfilled, I tell you that this is my last message. Previously the cup was filling up; now it is overflowing. Many cardinals, many bishops and many priests are on the road to perdition, bringing many souls with them. The Holy Eucharist is being given less importance.

We must avoid God's anger with us by our efforts at amendment. If we beg pardon with sincerity of soul, he will forgive us. I, your mother, through the intermediary of St. Michael the archangel, want to tell you to amend your lives. You are already receiving one of the last warnings. I love you very much and do not want your condemnation. Ask us sincerely and we will give to you. You should make more sacrifices. Think of the passion of Jesus.

Besides these two principal messages, several predictions were made at Garabandal. The most important had to do with the great punishment or *chastisement*. If it comes, it will fall upon the entire world. The visionaries are not allowed to say in what it will consist, but one of them, Conchita, declared that "it will be a result of the direct intervention of God, which makes it more terrible and fearful than anything we can imagine... When I saw it, I felt a great fear, even though at the same time I was seeing our Blessed Mother." "I have seen the chastisement," she said on another occasion. "I can assure that if it comes, it is worse than being enveloped in fire, worse than having fire above and beneath you." Jacinta adds that to her it appeared like fire falling from heaven. Such a prophecy naturally makes us think of nuclear warfare. However, Conchita has repeatedly declared that the Blessed Virgin says there will not be another world war.

Before the punishment, the world will be given a *warning*, in an effort to bring about conversion, so that the punishment can be averted. The warning too will come directly from God and be experienced by the entire world. Conchita says, "It will be like the revelation of our sins and will be seen and felt by everyone, believer and unbeliever alike, irrespective of whatever religion he may belong to. It will be seen and felt in all parts of the world and by every person." In 1987, when the Bishop of Santander lifted the ban on the celebration of Mass at Garabandal by visiting priests, as Conchita had predicted, she remarked simply, "The next event of Garabandal is the warning."

In order to convince people of the truth of the apparitions, God is going to work a great *sign* at Garabandal. It will be announced a week in advance, so that those who wish may go there. All who are there will see it. The sick will be healed and unbelievers converted. A permanent sign will remain thereafter, something that can be seen and photographed, but not touched.

Garabandal warned also of a time when the Church would be persecuted to such a point that it would seem to have disappeared. Priests would have to go into hiding and would have a difficult time saying Mass. The four girls had a vision of all this on the night of June 19, 1962. They saw multitudes of people suffering and screaming; and they themselves screamed with fear. The people who heard them were likewise terrified and began to pray earnestly. When the

people prayed, the children grew quieter; and the more ardent the prayer, the more peaceful were the children. Mary declared that the name of this "very great evil" was *communism.* How this relates to the chastisement is not fully clear.

The events predicted will take place in the following order: first, the Warning, next, the Sign, lastly, the Chastisement (unless it is averted by conversion).

In 1962, when Pope John XXIII died, Mary told Conchita that after Paul VI, there would be only three more popes. When Paul VI died, Mary reiterated that there would be only two more. After the short reign of John Paul I, Mary confirmed that

Conchita, twenty years after the apparitions

John Paul II is the last. She made it plain, however, that this did not mean that the end of the world was at hand, but only the end of "an era" - a term Conchita is unable to explain more precisely. It would seem from this that the events about which we are being warned cannot be put off into an indefinite future, but are due to begin very, very soon. Moreover, Conchita has a blind friend, Joey Lomangino of New York; and Mary has promised that Joey is going to receive his sight back when the miracle occurs.

San Damiano 1964-1981

Rosa Quattrini

In 1961, Mary appeared to an Italian woman named Rosa Quattrini, healed her from a long illness, and sent her to work for Padre Pio.[11] Three years later, Mary appeared to her again, and as a sign caused a pear tree to blossom in the month of October. For the rest of Rosa's life, each Friday during the recitation of the rosary at her house, Mary reappeared. She gave frequent messages, of which the following is typical:

My daughter ...You must announce to the world that everyone must pray because Jesus can no longer carry his cross. I want you all to be saved - all of you, both the good and the bad. I am the Mother of love, the Mother of all, and you, you are my children. This is why I want all of you to be saved.

I have come also to call the world to prayer because the chastisements are near.

---

[11] There is little available in English on San Damiano apart from J. Osee, *Call of the Virgin at San Damiano* (Christopher Publishing House, North Quincy, MA, 1977). For a more authoritative presentation, one may turn to the French study directed by Roland Maisonneuve and Michel de Belsunce, *San Damiano. Histoire et Documents* (Paris, Tequi, 2nd ed. 1989).

Medjugorje (1981...)

The visionaries during an apparition

The apparitions still taking place in the former Yugoslav village of Medjugorje[12] have become famous, partly because they occurred in a communist country, partly because anyone can go there and witness, if not the apparitions themselves, at least the ecstasy of the visionaries, and often the associated miracles. Moreover, most of the visionaries have visited this country.

As the story of Medjugorje is well known, and also very lengthy, we will give only a brief account here. Since June 25, 1981, the Queen of Peace, as she calls herself, has been appearing daily to

---

[12] The literature on Medjugorje is enormous. For the basic story, it is difficult to find a better introduction than *The Queen of Peace Visits Medjugorje* by Joseph Pelletier (Riehle Foundation, POB 7, Milford, OH 45150).

For a broader presentation of the story against its historical background and amid the controversies that have swirled around it, a detached, non-commital account has been given by Mary Craig in *Spark from Heaven* (Hodder and Stoughton, London, 1988; in the U.S.: Ave Maria Press, Notre Dame, IN).

Medjugorje: Facts, Documents, Theology, by Michael O'Carroll C.S.Sp. (3rd. ed. 1988, Veritas, Dublin) gives precisely what the title announces.

The fullest and most up-to-date information about Medjugorje is to be found in a series of writings by René Laurentin, published more or less annually in Paris by O.E.I.L., some of them published in English by Faith Publishing Co., Milford OH, 45150, e.g. *Nine Years of Apparitions - Toward Revelation of the Ten Secrets?*, 1990.

Medjugorje, the Message is a very readable and moving account filtered through the personal experience of the most famous of Medjugorje 'converts' - Wayne Weible (Paraclete Press, Orleans MA, 1989).

A spirited defense of the apparitions against critics has been assembled by Denis Nolan in *Medjugorje. A Time for Truth, a Time for Action* (Queenship Publishing Co. P.O.B. 42028, Santa Barbara, CA, 1993).

The messages of Our Lady at Medjugorje have been collected and presented by R. Laurentin and R. Lejeune in *Messages and Teachings from Medjugorje* (Riehle Foundation, Milford OH, 45150, 1988) and anonymously in *Words from Heaven* (St. James publishing, Birmingham AL, 1990).

several young people. Her message is that peace cannot be secured for the world until there is peace in the hearts of individuals; and that this requires a radical conversion through faith, prayer and fasting.

So far as prayer is concerned, Mary asks everyone to pray for an hour a day, and to say the complete rosary each day. As for fasting, she wants us to live every Friday on nothing but bread and water. Those unable to do this should fast in whatever way they can - and not only from food but from television, for example. Mary requested the formation in every parish of a prayer group that will pray for three hours daily and fast twice weekly. In fact, Medjugorje prayer groups have sprung up all over the world, especially in our country, and thousands of people have been brought to conversion or to a profound renewal of their Christian life through the Medjugorje message.

As at Garabandal, here too Mary has spoken of a great punishment that will come if mankind does not repent. It will be preceded by several warnings, and apparently will consist of at least two elements, which make the visionaries weep when they think of them. At Medjugorje too, a great sign will be worked to make people believe. Four of the youngsters know the date of this miracle, which they say will be very soon.

Mirjana, one of the visionaries, was told by Our Lady that God has given Satan power over the present century and that he, knowing that his time is short, is now acting with special ferocity to break up marriages and destroy religious vocations.

Betania: Maria Esperanza

Maria Esperanza

Of the numerous apparitions being reported today in Argentina, Ecuador, Puerto Rico, Nicaragua, Mexico and other Latin American countries, we can take note here only of one. The apparitions at Betania deserve attention because they are the first apparitions to receive official Church approval since those of Beauraing and Ban-neux in the 1930's. Betania is also remarkable because of the visionary, Maria Esperanza Medrano de Bianchini. In most of the other modern apparitions, the visionaries were generally just ordinary or even lukewarm Catholics, jerked out of their routine by an intervention of Mary that was doubly surprising because apparently quite unprepared for. But Maria Esperanza (born in 1928) had a lifetime of mystical experiences to prepare her for her mission. From childhood onwards she had been visited numerous times by St. Therese of Lisieux and the Blessed Mother. Her attempt to enter the religious life was thwarted by her heavenly visitors who 'arranged' her marriage to Geo Bianchin Gianni, whom she met in Rome. For a while, Padre Pio was her spiritual director; when he died, he appeared to her announcing that she was to follow in his path. In fact, she came to experience, not only such classical mystical phenomena as stigmata, levitation, the reading of people's hearts and the fragrance of roses, but also some very unusual ones such as her body being covered with a film of golden-hued moisture, and live roses growing out of her chest! And these things have been witnessed by doctors, lawyers, psychiatrists, engineers, atheists who have been converted by them, and even a TV journalist who filmed some of them.

It was in 1976 that Mary began appearing privately to Maria at Betania Finca, a small farm near Caracas, Venezuela. In 1984, on the feast of the Annunciation (March 25), the apparition itself was witnessed by a crowd of 108 people. By 1993, the number of witnesses to appari-

The Grotto at Betania Finca

tions at Betania was estimated between 1,000 and 2,000. Mary presents herself as "The reconciler of peoples and nations," and warns against the danger of terrible warfare if mankind does not accept the peace that comes from Christ. Although not many messages are given at Betania, Maria does warn of a terrible time of purification that is to come very soon, to be followed by a glorious coming of Our Lord, not to bring about the end of the world, but to introduce a paradisiac era of peace and love.

The bishop of Maria's diocese, Pio Bello Ricardo, although initially very skeptical, conducted a thorough investigation, personally interviewing the witnesses and collecting about 1,000 testimonies to the apparitions. On November 21, 1987, he issued an official declaration that, "in my judgment, these apparitions are authentic and of a supernatural character."[13]

Hrushiv

On April 27, 1987, one year to the day after the Chernobyl disaster, another Marian apparition was reported in the Ukrainian village of

Chapel of the Blessed Trinity

Hrushiv. At that time, Ukraine was still part of the Soviet Union, and the Communist regime was in full power. Despite vigorous efforts of the police to stop them, pilgrims came from all over the Union. The apparitions continued daily for three weeks, and the crowds sometimes surpassed 50,000. In contrast to other apparitions, Mary was seen and heard, not just by a few chosen visionaries, but by about half of the assembled people, as she hovered over the little wooden chapel of the Blessed Trinity which had been shut by the government some forty years earlier.[14]

Mary was often dressed in black, holding the infant Jesus in her arms. Here as elsewhere, she called for prayer and penance. She promised that Ukraine would be free within ten years (p. 266; in fact, Ukraine declared its independence in 1991). Mary added that the conversion of Russia would come about through the martyred people of Ukraine (271), but warned, **"If Russia does not accept Christ the king, the entire world faces ruin"** (271).

---

[13] This account is based on the book, *The Bridge to Heaven*, by Drew Mariani and Michael Brown (Marian Communications, POB 8, Lima PA, 1993).

[14] The only serious account of these apparitions in English is to be found in *The Witness*, by Joseph Terelya (Faith Publishing Co., POB 12317, Milford, OH 4515), chapters 1 and 17-21. References in the text are to this book.

"**I see fire,**" she said. "**The villages are burning. Water is burning. The very air is on fire. Everything is in flames, if people do not convert to Christ, there will be war. There shall be a great conflagration**" (269).

Weeping Madonnas

Besides apparitions, there have been other extraordinary Marian phenomena. In 1953, an image of the Blessed Virgin in Sicily shed tears for several days. The tear-shaped church erected to commemorate this event was consecrated on November 6, 1994, by Pope John Paul II. In the course of a moving meditation on the meaning of tears in Scripture, he likened Mary to "a mother crying when she sees her children threatened by a spiritual or physical evil."[15] Since then, many other images have wept, including the famous Pilgrim Statue of Fatima that is carried around the world, and the even more famous "Lady of Czestochowa." Perhaps the most important of these weeping Madonnas is a wooden statue of Mary in Akita, Japan,[16] which shed tears a hundred and one different times from 1974 to 1981. On one of these occasions it was photographed by a visiting missionary, and on another by Japanese television. Sometimes those tears were accompanied by blood. Meanwhile, Mary gave the following message to a nun, Sister Agnes Sasagawa Katsuko, who lives in the convent where the statue is kept:

> If men are not converted, the Father will let fall a great punishment on all mankind... This punishment will be worse than the flood, something that has never yet been seen. Fire will fall from Heaven.
>
> A large part of mankind will be destroyed by it. Priests will die along with the people. Those who are spared will have such great sufferings, they will envy those who died. The only weapon remaining will be the rosary and the sign left by (my) son.

---

[15] *Osservatore Romano*, Engl. ed. Nov. 16, 1994, p. 5.

[16] *Akita. The Tears and Message of Mary*, by Teiji Yashuda (101 Foundation, Asbury, NJ 08802-0151). My account is based chiefly upon the work, *J'ai Vu Pleurer Ma Mère à Akita (Japan)*, by Joseph-Marie Jacq (ed. Jules Hovine, 400 Av. J. Juarez, 59790 Ronchin, France).

Weeping and Streaming Madonnas

Above left: Sicily (1953)
Above right: Akita (1974...)
Below left: Montreal (1981...)
Below right: Korea (1985...)

See also the cover photo:
Chicago (1984), described in the preface

Pray the rosary every day. With it, pray for bishops and priests. The action of the devil has penetrated even into the church. Cardinals will oppose cardinals and bishops will oppose bishops. Priests who honor me will be ridiculed and combatted by their colleagues.

Altars and churches will be vandalized. The church will be filled with people ready to compromise. At the devil's instigation, many priests and religious will abandon their vocations. The demons will attack especially those who have offered themselves to the Father.

The loss of many souls is the reason for my sorrow...

Besides weeping statues, there have been images exuding fragrant or healing oil, such as the Portaissa ikon in Montreal or the little image of Mary belonging to Mirna Nazour in Damascus. There have likewise been bleeding statues, such as one in the possession of Julia Kim of Korea.

Berthe Petit

A life-long series of visions was given to a Belgian woman, Berthe Petit (1870-1943). Although it was Jesus rather than Mary whom she saw, the visions were largely concerned with Mary. The crucial one occurred in 1910, when Berthe saw the two hearts of Jesus and Mary fused into one, while Jesus said to her: **"You must think of my Mother's Heart as you think of mine; live in this heart as you would seek to live in mine; give yourself to this heart as you give yourself to mine. You must spread love of this heart so wholly united to mine."**

Berthe Petit

A few days later Berthe learned the mission to which she was to dedicate the rest of her life. Jesus said, **"The world must be dedicated to the Sorrowful and Immaculate Heart of my**

Mother, as it is dedicated to mine." Berthe had a vision of the entire world regenerated through this devotion.

From the First to the Second World War, Berthe received many revelations in advance about future events and about their hidden meaning. When the Archduke Ferdinand of Austria was assasinated in Sarajevo, Jesus said to her, **"Now begins the ascending curve of preliminary events which will lead to the great manifestation of my justice."**

When the Armistice was signed, he said:

> It will soon become apparent how unstable is a peace set up without me and without the intervention of him who speaks in my name [=the Holy Father]. The nation which is thought to be conquered, but whose strength is only temporarily diminished, remains a threat to your nation and to France.... Wars will blaze up again everywhere; civil wars, racial wars. What should have been so great, so true, so beautiful, so durable, is delayed....
>
> Humanity is rushing toward a dreadful storm which will divide the nations more and more, all human plans will be annihilated...

In 1922 he spoke of **"...the appalling cataclysm which approaches and which will overturn all the present calculations of mankind and their deplorable policies."**

In January of 1940, he told her, **"Belgium will be invaded."** This actually took place three months later. In 1941 he assured her that Belgium would again prosper, and that **"Deliverance will be the work of our two Hearts."**

Finally, in 1942, the year before her death, and two years before the first atom bomb fell on Hiroshima, Jesus said to Berthe, **"A frightful torment is in preparation. It will be seen that the forces launched in such fury will soon be let loose. Now or never is the moment for all of you to give yourselves to the Sorrowful Heart of my Mother.**

"By her acceptance of Calvary, my Mother has participated in all my sufferings. Devotion to her Heart united to mine will bring peace, that true peace so often implored and yet so little merited."

To represent this devotion, Berthe was directed by Our Lord to a picture venerated in the Benedictine convent of Ollignies, Belgium. In 1918, after the occupying troops had left the convent school, one of the nuns found in the basement a pornographic picture pasted onto a piece of cardboard. Tearing away the picture, she uncovered an image of Mary holding a lily in her left hand, while the right pointed to her sorrowful heart, pierced by a sword and enveloped in flames. The nuns put the picture in a place of honor and soon found that those who prayed before it obtained remarkable graces. Berthe and her associates had it reprinted for public distribution, accompanied by the invocation, **"O sorrowful and Immaculate Heart of Mary, pray for us who have recourse to you."**[17]

Father Gobbi (1972)

In addition to the apparitions and weeping statues, there are also certain chosen spokesmen through whom Mary has given messages for the world. The best known of these is Father Stefano Gobbi, a Pauline priest from Milan, Italy. Deeply troubled over the number of priests leaving their ministry, and of others who use their ministry as an occasion to undermine the Holy See, he made a pilgrimage to Fatima in 1972. There he was inspired to found the "Marian Union of Priests" who would consecrate themselves to the Immaculate Heart of Mary and pledge their faithful support of the Holy Father. In 15 years, without any propaganda, this Movement has spread all over the world.

---

[17] This section on Berthe Petit has been taken from the article, "Berthe Petit and the devotion to the Sorrowful and Immaculate Heart of Mary," by Joseph Pelletier A.A., in his book, *The Immaculate Heart of Mary* (Assumption Publications, Worcester MA, 1976).

WHY ALL THESE MARIAN APPARITIONS TODAY

One year later, Father Gobbi began to write down thoughts which seemed to have been inspired by Our Lady. His spiritual director urged him to gather them into a booklet which he submitted to the other priests for their appraisal. The booklet has won very wide recognition as containing authentic 'locutions' of the Blessed Virgin. Since then, a new edition has appeared every year or two, supplemented with more recent locutions, that now form a full length book, entitled, *To the Priests, Our Lady's beloved sons*.[18]

These 'words from Our Lady' consist mostly of spiritual counsels and encouragement. But they also provide a kind of commentary on the situation of the Church today. They interpret very accurately the message of the visions and other manifestations we have considered. The following are among their more important themes: First, the Church is now under fierce assault from Satan, who has created widespread confusion by inducing many priests to apostatize, others to rebel against authority, and others to promote false doctrine under the guise of a more enlightened belief. This situation will go on getting worse, until the light of Christ seems to have gone out, and Satan seems to have gained power over the whole world.

Second, the sufferings of the Church will culminate in a great chastisement. It is described in terms very similar to those used by some of the visionaries we have treated. For example, in 1986 Mary said:

> Because ... humanity has not accepted my repeated call
> to conversion, repentance and a return to God, there is
> about to fall upon it the greatest chastisement which
> the history of mankind has ever known. It is a chastise-
> ment much greater than that of the flood. Fire will fall
> from Heaven and a great part of humanity will be de-
> stroyed. (332)

---

[18] *To the Priests, Our Lady's Beloved Sons*, published by The Marian Movement of Priests, POB 8, St. Francis, ME, 04774-0008, 1990, followed by supplements for each of the years 1990, 1991, 1992 and 1993. References in the passages cited below are to the year and to the number used in this edition.

Third, it is through the Immaculate Heart of Mary that God will deliver the Church from this darkness and establish the Kingdom of Jesus her Son. Mary is already gathering an army of "little ones" led by priests devoted to her Immaculate Heart. Just when Satan seems to have conquered all, he will be overthrown. Mary says:

At the very moment when Satan is enthroned as Lord of the world and thinks himself now the sure victor, I my-self will snatch the prey from his hands. In a trice he will find himself empty-handed and in the end the victory will be exclusively my son's and mine. This will be the triumph of my Immaculate Heart in the world. (1973, #29)

Father Gobbi - or rather Mary speaking through him - assures us that afterwards, **"The desert of this world will be totally renewed by the merciful love of the Father.... The church and the world will thus be able to attain a splendor never before known."** (1978, #164)

You will see a New Earth and New Heavens.... The Father wants ... to mold with his hands a new creation where his imprint will be ... more visible, welcomed and received, and his fatherhood exalted and glorified...

... This creation will come back as a garden where Christ will be glorified, where his kingship will be welcomed and exalted. It will be a universal reign of grace, beauty, harmony, communion, sanctity, of justice and peace.

... The Holy Spirit will come down like a fire ... which burns and cleanses, transforms and sanctifies, which renews the earth from its very foundations, which opens hearts to a reality of life and brings souls to the fullness of holiness and of grace. (1987, #357 o-t)

Father Gobbi relates some of the events of our time to the prophecies of Fatima and Medjugorje. In 1984, on the Feast of the Annunciation, the day Pope John Paul consecrated the whole world to the Immaculate Heart, Mary said:

Today I renew my request that all be consecrated to my Immaculate Heart.

Before all, I ask it of my beloved son, Pope John Paul II, the first of my beloved sons who, on the occasion of this feast, performed the consecration in a solemn manner, after writing to the bishops of the world and inviting them to do so in union with him.

Unfortunately, this invitation was not welcomed by all the bishops; particular circumstances have not yet permitted the explicit consecration of Russia, which I have requested many times. As I have already told you, this consecration will be made to me when the bloody events are well on the way to actuality.

I bless this courageous act of my pope in his wish to entrust the world and all the nations to my Immaculate Heart; I receive it with love and gratitude and because of it I promise to intervene to shorten greatly the hours of the purification, and to lessen the gravity of the trial. (1984, #287)

On May 31 of that same year, Mary added:

Today, while you recall my first apparition which took place in Fatima in 1917, you are living the events I then predicted to you.

You are in the period in which the struggle between me, the woman clothed with the sun, and my adversary, the red dragon, is moving now towards its conclusion, and for this reason, I am again appearing in a new and more extraordinary way to assure you that my presence in your midst is habitual. (1984, #289)

During the Marian Year of 1987, Mary declared:

My times have arrived, beloved sons. These are my times.

. . .

Already during this Marian year, certain great events will take place, concerning what I predicted at Fatima

and have told, under secrecy, to the children to whom I
am appearing at Medjugorje. (1987, #357; cf. 355)

1987 was the year when Reagan and Gorbachev signed an agree-
ment about the non-proliferation of nuclear armaments, an act which
opened the way to the extraordinary series of events that have since
taken place in Eastern Europe. They signed this pact on December
8, the Feast of the Immaculate Conception.

Conclusion

Many other apparitions have been reported in the past decade and
a half which cannot be dealt with here. Some have been deliber-
ately passed over because they seem evidently spurious. Others I
am not well enough informed about to judge. There are simply too
many claims for a person to investigate them all carefully. But I
trust that I have given a representative selection of the more important and reliable ones.

Their meaning I have summed up in three points. First, Mary
comes as the smiling Madonna, to comfort, encourage and heal
her children. Secondly, she comes as an anxious mother, weeping
as she warns us that our Father is weary of our wickedness, that he
is about to punish us severely if we do not repent. Finally, she offers her *Immaculate Heart* as a refuge from the dangers that threaten,
and as the place where we can best learn to do the Father's will.

The message of encouragement is chief and most basic: it is
the front of the medal. In this report, I have somewhat emphasized
the note of warning, because that seems to be the reason for the
urgency of the message. Mary tells us that very little time is left for
us to reform our lives if we want to avert the threatened chastisement. This accounts for the extraordinary multiplication of apparitions in our time. Mary is a concerned mother, trying in every possible way, by every conceivable means, to touch the wayward hearts
of her children before it is too late. Through Father Gobbi, she
once declared that the reason for the multiplication of her miraculous manifestations in this century is that:

These are the times of the reign of my adversary, the
Red Dragon, Satan, the Old Serpent whose head I shall

crush. Under the weight of his reign, trials and sufferings, wounds and falls have increased for you, and thus the danger of being lost is much greater for all. And so I am manifesting myself to you in an extraordinary way to urge you to confidence, to trust, to take refuge in me through your act of consecration to my Immaculate Heart. (1988, #373)

This is not a message of doom and gloom, as is sometimes said. Not gloom, because the first word of the Queen of Peace is always one of encouragement, and her last one always an assurance of hope. Not doom, because her warnings are conditional: *If my people do not repent, they will suffer for their sins,* she says.

The ancient prophets were sent to warn Israel that God was weary of its crimes. Because Israel did not listen, its people were carried off into capitivity and its land was left desolate. Mary is like the prophet for our time, and we can thank the merciful heart of Jesus that he has sent us the sweetest and gentlest of all his prophets.

Some people object that these prophetic warnings sound more like the thundering of Yahweh in the Old Testament, than like the gentle word of the Father spoken by Jesus Christ. Anyone who says that must not be very familiar with the New Testament. Merciful Savior though Jesus was, he could also be unsparing in his warnings. When told how Pilate had slaughtered some people who were offering sacrifice to the Lord, Jesus commented, "Unless you repent, you will all perish in the same way" (Luke 13:3) To the towns that did not listen to his preaching, he declared, "Woe to you Korazin! Woe to you, Bethsaida! It will be more bearable for Tyre and Sidon on the day of judgment than for you. And you, Capernaum, will you be lifted up to the heavens? No, you will go down into Hades" (Matthew 11:20 ff.) The Book of Apocalypse becomes almost monotonous in its reiteration of severe warnings delivered by Jesus through the apostle John. If Jesus could speak thus through the Beloved Disciple, surely he can do likewise through the Blessed Virgin. And when Mary weeps over the state of the world, that is hardly incompatible with Jesus weeping over Jerusalem when he foresaw that not one stone would be left standing on another (Luke 19:41 f.).

What most disturbs some people about the Marian apparitions is the vivid prediction of impending catastrophes. Many apocalyptic prophets in the past have predicted doomsday for their own time and subsequently looked very foolish. May not Akita's description of fire falling from heaven, or Garabandal's reference to the last of the popes, be destined for a similar fate?

Indeed we need to be cautious about the claims of extraordinary supernatural phenomena. But all of the apparitions discussed in this paper have very serious grounds of credibility. Many have received official approbation by the Church after a careful examination: the Miraculous Medal, La Salette, Lourdes, Fatima, Beauraing and Akita. The others are all backed up by weighty evidence, which there is not space to go into here.

Even authentic apparitions and prophecies are not to be put on the same level as Sacred Scripture. Though divinely inspired, they are not always immune from error, due to the human beings through whom they are delivered. It is right, therefore, to be reserved about concrete details, even when the prophet seems to be genuine. But we must not forget that many of the specific things predicted in the Marian apparitions have already come true: the French Revolution of 1830, the famine of 1847, the two world wars, the spread of atheistic communism, and many other details. There is very serious evidence that the conversion of Russia, which Mary foretold seventy years ago, may now be under way. These fulfillments give us grounds to take the other warnings seriously, even when they go into detail.

If there is weighty reason to believe that the Mother of Jesus has appeared and spoken in our world, we had better take her seriously. It is surely not for any trivial matter that Jesus sends her to appeal to us. If we disregard her, are we not in danger of hearing him repeat to us what he said to Jerusalem, "You did not recognize the time of your visitation" (Lk 19:44)? But if, like Elizabeth, we appreciate what a great grace it is for the Mother of the Lord to come to us, may we not expect that the sound of her voice will bring us too a new infilling of the Holy Spirit?

In any case, the principal theme of Mary's message is neither the chastisement, nor the blessed age that is to follow it, but her Immaculate Heart. This she offers as a shelter against the evil of this world that seeks to corrupt us, as a refuge in the coming chastisement, and as the place where we can be formed by her as brothers and sisters of Jesus.

Nearly 300 years ago, St. Louis de Montfort affirmed that the Kingdom of Christ would come about through the queenship of

Mary; that just as Jesus came into the world through her in his physical body, and as he now comes into our lives by grace through her mediation, so it is through her that he will bring about his final reign. In order to help bring this about, St. Louis urged everyone to be consecrated to her.

Mary's messages today seem to suggest that we are now living through some of the great moments of the realization of St. Louis' prophecy. However, we are not invited to be mere spectators at this drama. We are summoned to take an active part in it; to belong to the army that Mary is now gathering to attack her Adversary. In another text

St. Louis de Montfort

from Father Gobbi, she says:

> I, the little "handmaid of the Lord," shall place myself at the head of a great company of the humble to attack the stronghold manned by the proud. The only thing I ask of all my sons is that they consecrate themselves to my Immaculate Heart; that they let themselves be possessed by me. (1977, #127)

Far more than mere soldiers to help in the triumph of Mary's Immaculate Heart, we are invited to be the very beginning of her reign; for she says:

> When the first buds appear on the trees, you say that winter is coming to an end and that a new spring is near. I have pointed out to you the sign of the cruel winter

through which the Church is now passing in the purification which has become so painful...

But see how, in her worst winter, the buds of a renewed life are beginning to appear.... For the Church, a new springtime of the triumph of my Immaculate Heart is about to issue forth. She will still be the same Church, but a Church renewed, illumined, made humbler, stronger, poorer and more evangelical by its purification....

Many new buds may already be seen sprouting on her branches; these are all those who have had confidence in their heavenly Mother -you, Apostles of my Immaculate Heart. You are these buds, my little children, who are consecrated to me and who live by my own spirit. (1979, #172)

WHY ALL THESE MARIAN APPARITIONS TODAY

Appendix

Three Days of Darkness

Brother David at St. Mary's College, Notre Dame, January 17, 1995

During the past two hundred years, mystics have occasionally made reference to a terrible "three days of darkness" which the world would one day undergo.[19] It is not always evident how these prophecies relate to the Marian messages given above; but in the words of a recent spokesman, Brother David Lopez O.S.F. of El Ranchito, Texas, the three days of darkness are like the "outer wrapping" of the chastisement.[20]

Brother David had a kind of interior vision of these days on August 15, 1987, while praying the rosary with the crowd at Medjugorje. He heard the voice of Mary saying:

Do not be afraid about the three days of darkness that will come over the earth, because those who are living my messages and have an interior life of prayer will be alerted by an interior voice three days to one week before their occurrence.

My children must continue with repentance for their sins and pray more, as I have recommended. They should get holy water and blessed articles, and have special devotion to the Sacred Heart of Jesus, having always a

---

[19] Cf. *The Three Days' Darkness* by Father Albert Hebert (POB Paulina, 70763, 1986). Unfortunately, this work gives so few references, it is difficult to check its accuracy.

[20] In a private conversation, January 15, 1995.

vigil light in front of him. They must be content with satisfying the basic necessities of life and be less dependent on material goods.

The priests must not only take care of their own interior life, but also develop the interior prayer life of all their parishioners. The same way they should avoid anyone who speaks about revolution and rebellion. The ones who speak about revolution and rebellion are the disciples of the Antichrist.

I am sad for the religious of the West who have renounced their signs of consecration. They, especially, will be tempted by Satan and will not be able to resist the spiritual and physical attacks. They must return to a life of sanctity and obedience to Christ, my Son.

But Mary concluded her message with words of reassurance:

Do not be afraid of anything or anybody. Be filled with God's love by praying, reading Holy Scripture and receiving the sacraments. I will be with you during the time of anguish, and my children may call on me for secure refuge.

Those who are struggling to overcome recurring personal sin should not despair because God will take into account their desires and efforts to conquer their sins. Go in peace.

At the same time as he heard these words, Brother David had "impressions" (elsewhere called by him an interior understanding) that went beyond Mary's words, giving details that accord with many of the nineteenth century prophecies (which David had not read). The darkness will be so great, he says, we will not be able to see our own hands or faces. It will last exactly 72 hours. All the demons of hell will be let loose on the earth. Those "who are not in the state of grace are going to die of fright because of the horrible demons they will see." We should stay in our homes, keeping windows and doors locked, and not respond to calls from outside (where the demons will imitate the voices of our loved ones, trying to lure us out of the house).

There will be no electricity during those days. In an obvious allusion to Matthew 24:19, 20, Mary said to pray that these events not occur in winter, for no heat will be available; pray also that there be no women pregnant then, for they will have no medical assistance. Those days will be especially difficult for solitary people, for which reason, **"it is very important to form communities of fraternal alliances where you can have support from your brothers."** On the other hand, the prayers of children will be miraculous.

"Before the great tribulation. . .we will see in the sky one great red cross on a day of blue sky without clouds." It will be seen by everyone, and even non-Christians will understand its significance if they have listened to the voice of God in the sanctuary of their hearts. Some people will be martyred at the beginning of the three days, and will be taken body and soul to heaven.

After the days of darkness there will be a kind of spring time. "Everything will be green, everything will be clean. The water will be crystal clear, even the water from the faucets in the houses. There will be no contamination in the water, nor the air, nor the river" (referring to the Rio Grande, beside which Brother David's hermitage is situated).

WHY ALL THESE MARIAN APPARITIONS TODAY

– II –
FATHER GOBBI
ON THE END TIMES

Father Gobbi at Effingham, Illinois, 1994

The visionaries and locutionaries examined in the preceding chapter have, as a group, insisted that the state of the world today is very grave. The Lord is calling us to repentance, for want of which we will undergo a severe chastisement. The assurance that this is to be followed by a radical restoration only emphasizes the momentous character of these times. There are interpreters, however, who go even further, claiming that we are entering into the Apocalyptic era - not "apocalyptic" in the rhetorical sense that refers simply to mighty upheavals, but "Apocalyptic" in reference to the final age of the world as announced in various texts of Scripture.

The best known and perhaps best accredited of these interpreters is Father Gobbi, some of whose messages have already been cited in chapter 1.[21] His doctrine is also presented in far richer detail

---

[21] Father Gobbi's writings are to be found in the work, *To the Priests, Our Lady's Beloved Sons*, published by The Marian Movement of Priests, P.O.B. 8, St. Francis ME 04774-0008. The principal volume contains the messages from 1973 through 1989. Supplements have been published for the years 1990, 1991, 1992 and 1993. References will be given by year and by the number of the message; thus 1990, #420b means, "Message #420, given in the year 1990 paragraph b."

than that of most others, who usually make only rather brief and general references to "the chastisement" or "the reign of Anti-christ" or the like.[22] Because of the difficulty in discerning among so many claimants those that are worthy of serious consideration, their texts will not be cited here. Anyone who wishes to get an idea of them can do so readily by reading a few issues of the review, *Signs of Our Times*.[23]

When, in the passages that follow, I refer to Mary speaking through Father Gobbi, I am adopting as my own the conviction shared by many, many readers that his book does indeed contain locutions received from Our Lady. Justification of this would require a long, critical study, which cannot be undertaken here. In order to avoid tedious repetition, however, I will sometimes simply cite Father Gobbi.

Apocalypse unsealed

His 'Apocalyptic' outlook is well summed up in the following message:

The Holy Spirit will make you understand the signs of your time. They are the times foretold by Holy Scripture as those of the great apostasy and of the coming of the Antichrist. They are times of great tribulation and of innumerable sufferings for all, which will bring you to live through these final events in preparation for the second coming of Jesus in glory. (1991, #450)

In 1987, Mary summoned "all" to look at **"the Book which is still sealed,"** adding that **"today I am being sent by God to open**

---

[22] An exception is Vassula Ryden, whose vision remarkably parallels that of Father Gobbi. I would have wished to compare the two of them here; but out of deference to the Congregation for the Doctrine of the Faith, which severely criticized Vassula in a "Notification" of October 6, 1995, and also for fear of compromising Father Gobbi, I will omit all but a few of the more interesting comparisons between them.

[23] Edited by Maureen Flynn, 109 Executive Drive Suite D, Sterling VA 20166.

this Book, in order that the secrets may be revealed to you" (366g).[24] On the last day of that same year, Mary repeated:

> With my motherly voice I am leading you all to understand *the signs of the great tribulation*. From the gospels, from the Letter of the Apostles and from the Book of the Apocalypse, sure signs have been clearly described for you to make you understand what the period of the great tribulation is. All these signs are in the act of being realized in this time of yours (370c).

A warning from history

History teaches us to be wary of apocalyptic prophets. The first generation Christians seem to have expected Jesus to return in their own time. In 601, St. Gregory the Great, writing to the English king Ethelbert, pointed out indications that "the end time is near." Five hundred years later, Hugh of St. Victor (d. 1141) still felt that the end was not far off. In 1255, the superiors general of the Dominicans and Franciscans wrote a joint letter declaring that God had raised up their two communities "in the last days, at the

St. Gregory the Great writing under the inspiration of the Holy Spirit
(from the *Book of Hours* of Jean, Duke of Berry)

---

[24] The book referred to here is the Apocalypse, according to Father Gobbi (in a private conversation of October 11, during a retreat preached by him at Effingham, IL.). As early as 1980, Mary had already said, **"I am the Virgin of the Apocalypse... I will bring you to the full understanding of Sacred Scripture. Above all, I will read to you the pages of its last book, which you are living. In it, everything is already predicted, even that which must still come to pass. The battle to which I am calling you is clearly described, and my great victory is foretold"** (1980, #198c,h). It is interesting to note that Vassula too speaks of a sealed book that is now being opened, but for her it is the Old Testament apocalypse - the book of Daniel. (Message of Dec. 20, 1993; *True Life in God*, Trinitas edition, Independence MO, vol. VII, p. 65ff).

end of the world, as we believe without any doubt." In 1412, St. Vincent Ferrer could still argue that the Antichrist would come very soon, to be followed almost immediately by the end of the world.[25] In our own country, William Miller, founder of the Seventh-Day Adventists, predicted that all would end in 1843-1844, a date later revised by Jonathan Cummings to 1854.[26] I personally remember a Pentecostal preacher assuring me in 1970 that the Lord's coming would occur before his rickety car gave out. More recently, the radio evangelist Harold Camping announced that the Day of Judgment would almost certainly fall between September 15 and 27 of 1994.[27] And who could count all the groups which, led by the enthusiasm of some now-forgotten prophet, have given away their possessions and gone out on a hill-top to await the end?[28]

---

[25] All these texts, and others like them, can be found in *Visions of the End*, by Bernard McGinn (New York, Columbia U.P., 1979). More examples, ancient, mediaeval and modern, can be found in *Antichrist and the Millennium* by E. R. Chamberlin (New York, Dutton, 1975). But the reader should be cautioned that this lively account adopts an attitude of completely secular skepticism in treating the biblical texts. In dealing with later history, it puts the author's imaginative reconstructions on the same level as historical facts. Other late mediaeval examples will be cited below, in chapter 5.

My manuscript had already gone to the publisher when I learned of Bernard McGinn's new book, *Antichrist: Two Thousand Years of Fascination with Evil* (Harper-Collins, 1995), too late for me to use it.

[26] Cf. John Hardon, *The Protestant Churches of America*, Image Book edition 1969, pp. 29f.

[27] Cf. *New York Times*, December 31, 1994, p. 7. For anyone who would like to have more examples of this sort, there is even a review available: *Millenial Prophecy Report*, published by Ted Daniels, POB 34021, Philadelphia PA 19101-4021.

[28] St. Ephraem of Syria accurately expressed the state of the question as early as 365-370, when he observed that, "although he [Jesus] has given [an indication of] the signs of his coming, we do not know when they terminate. They have come and gone amid constant changes, and they are still present.... [The Lord] pointed out these signs so that from that day forward all peoples and ages might think that his coming would take place in their own day." (*Commentary on the Diatesseron*, ch. 18, #15, 16. My translation is based mainly on that of *Sources Chrétiennes* vol. 121, pp. 325-327. The original text can be found in *Corpus Scriptorum Christianorum Orientalium*, vol. 137-145, pp. 189-190. There is an English translation by Carmel McCarthy in the *Journal of Semitic Studies*, Supplement 2, Oxford U. Press, 1993, pp. 278-280).

Because of such experiences, I have always been very skeptical of end-time prophets. Nevertheless, the personal credentials of Father Gobbi, and the luminosity of his insights into the state of our times, convince me that, on the present topic also, his message deserves to be taken very seriously.

The principal texts

In interpreting our times, he refers principally to two texts of Scripture besides the Apocalypse. One is from the long answer Jesus gave when the apostles asked for signs of the destruction of the Temple and his return. Seated on the Mount of Olives, overlooking the Temple which was the focal point of the Jewish religion, Jesus said:

> When you see the desolating abomination spoken of through Daniel the prophet [=Dan. 12:11] standing in the holy place (let the reader understand), then those in Judea must flee to the mountains... At that time there shall be great tribulation such as has not been from the beginning of the world until now, nor ever will be.

After a warning against false prophets, the passage continues:

> Immediately after the tribulation of those days, the sun will be darkened and the moon will not give its light... And then the sign of the Son of Man will appear in the heavens... (Matthew 24:15-30)

The second text is from St. Paul's Second Letter to the Thessalonians. In squelching rumors that the Day of the Lord had already come, Paul declared that the "apostasy" must come first, and the "lawless one" (also translated "the man of lawlessness") must be revealed:

> The mystery of lawlessness is already at work. But the one who restrains is to do so only for the present, until he is removed from the scene. And then the lawless one will be revealed, whom the Lord Jesus will kill with the

breath of his mouth and render powerless by the manifestation of his coming. (2:7-8)

St. Paul nowhere uses the name *Antichrist*, but "the lawless one" seems to be an equivalent expression. Paul describes this person as "the one doomed to perdition, who opposes and exalts himself above every so-called god and object of worship, so as to seat himself in the temple of God, claiming that he is a god" (II Thes. 2:3-4). Finally, St. Paul reminds his readers that he has already told them these things while still with them (v. 5), and adds the tantalizing remark, "And now you know what is restraining, that he may be revealed in his time" (v. 6).

The terms *tribulation*, *desolating abomination*, *apostasy*, *lawless one*, and *what is restraining* (or *the one who restrains*), taken from the two texts cited, come up repeatedly in the messages of Father Gobbi. They are at times mingled together so inextricably that it is not possible to treat them separately, but we can begin with the apostasy.

The Apostasy

Father Gobbi insists that the apostasy foretold by St. Paul (and in different terms by Jesus in Luke 18:8) has already begun in the Church today:

> In these times, errors are spreading more rapidly and profoundly than you can imagine. Many are losing the faith and apostasy is expanding more and more within the Church, like a terrible cancer which has spread through all its members. (1991, #448)

> Satan has succeeded in entering into the Church, the New Israel of God. He has entered there with the smoke of error and sin, of the loss of faith and apostasy, of compromise with the world and the search for pleasure. During these years, he has succeeded in leading astray bishops and priests, religious and faithful....

You are living the bloody years of the battle, because the great trial has now arrived for all. (1993, #495)

Usually an apostate means someone who rejects the faith and leaves the Church. In these texts, however, apostasy consists rather in a distortion or corruption of the Christian faith, which is all the more serious when it is the work of those whose office it is to proclaim and defend the faith. Father Gobbi expresses it thus in a message given in Brazil:

> The Church here is running into a grave danger, that of becoming a victim of apostasy and loss of the true faith. The dangers which are threatening her are those of contestation, division, and numerous and public criticisms which are directed at the Pope and his Magisterium on the part of some bishops, priests, religious and faithful. (1990, #419)

> You read in the gospel, "When the Son of Man returns will He still find faith on earth?" [Lk 18:8]... They are grave words, which cause one to reflect and which succeed in making you understand the times through which you are living. First of all, you can ask why Jesus has uttered them: to prepare you for his second coming and to describe for you a circumstance which will be indicative of the proximity of his glorious return.

This circumstance is the loss of faith.

> Also, in another part of Holy Scripture, in the letter of Saint Paul to the Thessalonians, it is clearly announced that, before the glorious return of Christ, a great apostasy must take place. The loss of the faith is a true apostasy. The spread of the apostasy is therefore the sign which indicates that the second coming of Christ is, as of now, close at hand. (1990, #420)

Predicted at Fatima

Mary has several times indicated to Father Gobbi that this loss of faith had been predicted at Fatima:

> At Fatima, I have foretold to you that a time would come when the true faith would be lost. These are the times. (1990, #420)[29]

In the published words of Our Lady at Fatima, there is no such statement. However those who have tried to decipher the contents of the famous "third part" of the secret of Fatima, which has never been published, have sometimes concluded (especially on the basis of Our Lady's words, "in Portugal the dogma of the faith will always be preserved,") that the secret had to do with a widespread loss of faith or apostasy in the Church. Thus, Father Joaquin Alonso, C.M.F., for many years the official archivist of Fatima, expressed the opinion that it referred to a crisis of faith. A detailed study by Frère Michel de la Trinité, reiterates this conclusion, adding, "Such a crisis of faith on a scale encompassing various nations or entire continents has a name in Holy Scripture: namely, *apostasy*."[30] This view is also seconded by Cardinal Oddi,[31] René Laurentin and others.[32] Father Gobbi has expressly confirmed[33] that the text just cited does indeed refer to the third part of the Fatima secret.

---

[29] On another occasion, Mary referred to "the prophecy which was given to you by me at Fatima, that the times will come when many will lose the true faith" (1989, #406 1). Likewise: "There is now taking place that which is contained in the third part of my message, which has not yet been revealed to you, but which has now become evident from the events themselves through which you are now living" (1993, #495, in a message given on May 13, recalling the Fatima apparitions).

[30] Michel de la Trinité, *Toute la Vérité Sur Fatima - Le Troisième Secret*, Contre-Réforme Catholique, Saint-Parres-Les-Vaudes, 1985, pp. 461f.

[31] See interview in *Il Sabato* magazine, March 17, 1990, E.T. in *The Fatima Crusader*, Summer, 1990, p. 14f.

[32] An article signed "J.P." in the *Fatima Crusader* lists Father Martins dos Reis, Canon Galamba, Mgr. Venancio, Father Luis Kondor, and Father Messias Dias Coelho.

[33] In a private conversation of Oct. 11, 1994.

"The One who restrains"

In speaking about the apostasy that is to come, St. Paul alludes also to "the one who restrains" (II Thes. 2:7). Father Gobbi identifies this mysterious personage as Pope John Paul II.[34] After calling the Pope, **"this precious gift which my Immaculate Heart has made to you,"** Mary added:

> Today I confirm for you that *this is the Pope of my secret*; the Pope about whom I spoke to my children during the apparitions.... The Pope gives to all the light of Christ, in these times of great darkness .... When this Pope has completed the task which Jesus has entrusted to him and I come down from Heaven to receive His sacrifice, all of you will be cloaked in a dense darkness of apostasy, which will then become general. (1991, #449)[35]

This accords eerily with the Garabandal message that John Paul II will be the last pope.[36] Father Gobbi goes so far as to suggest that the Holy Father will be assassinated:

> Those who are making attempts upon his [the Pope's] life are on the point of carrying out their dark design. At this time, the hour of Calvary and of his personal immolation is close (1987, #359d).

---

[34] Vassula makes the same identification, for example, in the message of Dec. 20, 1993 (*True Life in God*, VII, p. 66). Note, however, that this need not be taken in the sense that St. Paul himself was referring to the Pope. What Paul had in mind we do not know; but God, the ultimate author of Scripture, could intend references that went beyond the ken of the human author. Thus, in Hosea (11:1), "Out of Egypt I called my son" referred to the people of Israel; but Matthew 2:15 recognizes it as applying to Jesus.

[35] The text goes on, however, to give the comforting reassurance: **"There will remain faithful only that little remnant which, in these years by accepting my motherly invitation, has let itself be enfolded in the secure refuge of my Immaculate Heart. And it will be the little faithful remnant, prepared and formed by me, that will have the task of receiving Christ, who will return to you in glory, bringing about in this way the beginning of the new era which awaits you."**

[36] See chapter 1.

The "desolating abomination"

The prophet Daniel speaks about a "desolating abomination" (Dan. 9:27, 11:31; 12:11; cf. I Mac. 1:54), referring apparently to a statue or altar of Zeus that had been erected in the Hebrew temple by the Syrian king, Antiochus Epiphanes, who likewise put a stop to the daily sacrifice offered there by the Jews. When the apostles asked Jesus what sign there would be of his coming and of the end of the age, Jesus responded by referring to "the desolating abomination spoken of through Daniel the prophet standing in the holy place" (Mat. 24:3, 15). This translation is from the New American Bible (revised); other translations are: "the abomination that makes desolate" [RSV], "the abomination that causes desolation" [NIV], "the abomination of desolation" [Douay-Rheims, King James], "an appalling abomination" [Anchor Bible], "horrible abomination" [NAB] and "the awful horror" [TEV].) Father Gobbi refers frequently to this same reality under the name, "horrible sacrilege." In listing the signs of "the end of times" (to be discussed below), he says:

> The fourth sign is the horrible sacrilege, perpetrated by him who sets himself against Christ, that is, the Antichrist. He will enter into the Holy Temple of God and will sit on His throne, and have himself adored as God. (1992, #485o)

In identifying the "horrible sacrilege," the Blessed Mother refers Father Gobbi to Daniel 12:9-12. She identifies the nature of this sacrilege as a theology which:

> ... seeks to attack the ecclesial devotion towards the sacrament of the Eucharist. It gives value only to the meal aspect, tends to minimize its sacrificial value, seeks to deny the real and personal presence of Jesus in the consecrated host (1989, #406q).

In other words, the naturalistic interpretation of the Eucharist as primarily a banquet celebrated by the Christian community - a notion widespread in today's Church - will one day replace the authentic sense of the Sacrifice of the Mass and the Real Presence. In this will consist the infamous "horrible sacrilege."[37]

The idol which has already begun to be set up in the temple of the human spirit is a false mentality composed of such elements as Rebellion, Rationalism, Naturalism and atheistic self-sufficiency.

Summary

In sum, Father Gobbi holds that we have already entered into the apostasy which will culminate in the Antichrist. This apostasy, which consists in a mentality marked particularly by naturalism and rationalism, is being held back by Pope John Paul II. When he has been taken out of the way, the apostasy will become general, and will be characterized particularly by a humanistic counterfeit replacing the authentic Eucharist.

Masonry

Numerous details from the Apocalypse are interpreted as referring to contemporary events, especially from 1989 onwards. Father Gobbi had already been saying for years that the great red dragon of Apocalypse 12:3 represented Marxist atheism (cf. 1973, #28; 1989, #404). In 1989 he added that the beast arising out of the sea (Apoc 13:1) was Freemasonry (404); and the beast that comes up out of the earth (Apoc 13:11), ecclesiastical Masonry (406),

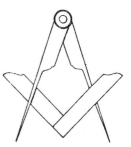

Masonic emblem:
The compass and square

---

[37] Vassula has a similar interpretation for what, in her terms, is called "the disastrous abomination": **"The** *disastrous abomination* **installed inside My Temple... is: the spirit of Rebellion that claims to be My equal; it is the spirit of Evil that enthroned itself in My sanctuary taking the place of My Perpetual Sacrifice, turning your generation Godless; it is the spirit of Rationalism and of Naturalism that led most of you into atheism; this is the spirit that makes you believe you are self-sufficient and that you can achieve** *everything* **by your own efforts and by your own strength; this disastrous abomination turned you into a waterless country of drought, a desert; My Perpetual Sacrifice you have abolished from within you because you have lost your faith..."** (June 6, 1991; *True Life in God,* IV, p. 163).

which, he says, **"Has spread especially among members of the hierarchy"** (406g). The latter beast has two horns, which Father Gobbi relates to the two peaks of a bishop's mitre (406g).

> The forces of Masonry have entered into the Church, in a subtle and hidden way, and have set up their stronghold in the very place where the vicar of my Son Jesus lives and works. (1993, #495)

Ordinary Masonry leads people to worship false gods; "ecclesiastical Masonry" fosters a false concept of Christ and the Church (1989, #406g). Whereas Jesus is the Way, the Truth and the Life, Masonry opposes his Truth **"By means of natural and rational** [that is to say, "naturalistic and rationalistic"?] **interpretations"** which, in attempting to make his divine word **"more understandable and acceptable, empty it of all its supernatural content"** (1989, #406, 1). It opposes the Life of grace by **"justifying sin,... presenting it no longer as an evil but as something good and of value"** with the consequence that **"it is no longer necessary to confess it."** As a result, individual confession has disappeared everywhere (#406m). Whereas Jesus is the Way to the Father, **"Ecclesiastical Masonry favors those forms of exegesis which give it a rationalistic and natural interpretation, with the result of denying the historical reality of miracles and of the resurrection,"** as well as placing **"in doubt the very divinity of Jesus and His salvific mission"** (#406n).

Ecclesiastical Masonry likewise distorts the Church:

> ... through *false ecumenism*, which leads to the acceptance of all christian Churches, asserting that each one of them has some part of the truth. It develops the plan of founding a universal ecumenical church, formed by the fusion of all the Christian confessions, among which, the Catholic Church. (#406p)

Whereas the Church gives life through the sacraments, above all the Eucharist, ecclesiastical Masonry replaces the Sacrifice of the Mass and the Real Presence of Christ with a naturalistic community celebration, as we have seen above. This leads in turn to the suppression of external marks of faith, **"such as genuflections, hours of public adoration and the holy custom of surrounding the tabernacle with lights and flowers"** (406q). Finally, ecclesiastical Masonry seeks to destroy the Church's unity by attacks on the Holy Father, the foundation of unity (406r).

Many American readers will be surprised at the way Masonry is singled out by Father Gobbi as the principal enemy of Christianity. In this country, Masonry is generally thought of as a benevolent social organization. However, in Europe, where it originated during the eighteenth century, Masonry has retained more of its original anti-Catholic spirit. There are moreover authors who maintain that, even in America, this spirit has not diminished but has only been concealed. I have not the information to make any judgment on this point, and am merely presenting the teaching which Father Gobbi transmits from the Blessed Virgin.[38] Neither have I ever heard of any avowed Masons among the clergy. However, the naturalistic humanism described above harmonizes well with the Masonic ideal of a morality based, not on any revelation or dogma, but simply on the notion of "Humanity." If this is what Father Gobbi means by ecclesiastical Masonry, it is widespread among theologians and has certainly affected some of the hierarchy.

Other details

Father Gobbi identifies the first of the seven plagues of Apocalypse 15-16 as AIDS (1989, #412). Apocalypse 12:14 speaks of the two wings of the great eagle given to the woman clothed with the sun to enable her to escape from the dragon. The eagle, Gobbi says, is the Word of God, especially as contained in the Gospel, above all that of John (1989, #403 d,e). The three angels of Apocalypse 14 are interpreted as announcing, (1) **"the defeat of Satan and of every diabolical spirit"**; and (2 & 3) *"the great chastisement* **meted out to those who have allowed themselves to be drawn away by sin and evil..."** (1992; §478j,n,o). The chain by which Satan is to be bound for a thousand years (Apoc. 20:1) is the

---

[38] Vassula likewise declares that "the beast of Apocalypse 13:1-18 represents Freemasonry." (Her footnote to the message of December 12, 1993; *True Life of God*, VII, p. 68.)

rosary (1992, §479n-t). Mary invites us to lift up our eyes to heaven today, because the great Rider, "King of kings and Lord of lords," is about to appear there (1992, 480j).

666

Of all the Apocalyptic interpretations made by Father Gobbi, the most difficult for most people to accept may be that of the number 666, the number of the Beast (Apoc. 13:18). After proposing that 333 represents the mystery of God (most obviously as Trinity), he affirms that 666 represents the one who wants to put himself above God. Then he goes on to say that, taken once, it stands for the year 666 - the period of history when the Antichrist was being manifested through Islam. Taken twice, it designates the year 1332, when Antichrist was at work through:

> ... a radical attack on faith in the word of God. Through the philosophers who begin to give exclusive value to science and then to reason, there is a gradual tendency to constitute human intelligence alone as the sole criterion of truth.

Taken three times, 666:

> ... expresses the year 1998... In this period of history, Freemasonry, assisted by its ecclesiastical form, will succeed in its great design: that of setting up an idol to put in the place of Christ and of his Church. A false christ and a false church. Consequently, the statue built in honor of the first beast, to be adored by all the inhabitants of the earth and which will seal with its mark all those who want to buy or sell [Apoc 13:14-17], is that of the *Antichrist*. You have thus arrived at the peak of the purification, of the great tribulation and of the apostasy... then the door will be open for the appearance of the man or of the very person *of the Antichrist* (1989, #407i-p).[39]

---

[39] Earlier in this same message, Father Gobbi declares that, "Lucifer, the ancient serpent, the devil or Satan, the Red Dragon, becomes, in these last times, the Antichrist.... The statue or idol, built in honor of the beast to be adored by all men, is the Antichrist" (407j).

The Antichrist

The Antichrist is apparently understood at various levels by Father Gobbi as Satan, as anyone who denies Christ, as the false image of Christ and the Church proposed by "ecclesiastical Masonry" and finally, as a particular person who is yet to come.

Tribulation, chastisement, purification

The distinction and inter-relations of what are called *tribulation*, *chastisement* and *purification* are not always evident. They seem to refer to realities that are closely related, yet somewhat distinct. It would seem that the tribulation foretold by Jesus in Matthew 24:21 is now underway, whereas the chastisement will take place in the future. According to Father Gobbi, the New Testament gave many signs by which the tribulation could be recognized, all of which are being realized in the present age: the apostasy, **"overturning of the order of nature... such as earthquakes, droughts, floods, and disasters which cause the unforeseen death of thousands of persons, followed by epidemics and incurable diseases which are spreading everywhere," "continual rumors of wars... conflicts and dissensions within countries....," "great signs in the sun, on the moon and in the stars,"** beginning with the miracle at Fatima and continuing in the miracle of the sun observed at so many apparition sites.

> ...these great signs which are taking place in your time are telling you that even now there has come to you the great tribulation which is preparing you for the new era which I have promised you with the triumph of my Immaculate Heart in the world. (1987, #370)

Father Gobbi uses *purification* almost as a synonym for the tribulation, to designate its role in preparing the world for the New Heavens and the New Earth. Hence Mary can say, **"This decisive time of the purification and the great tribulation is the time of the Holy Spirit"** (1933, #496d). The chastisement, which lies in the future, will be the culmination of the purification:[40]

---

[40] From a private conversation of October 11, 1994.

Humanity will know the bloody hour of its chastisement; it will be stricken with the scourge of epidemics, of hunger and of fire; much blood will be spilt upon your roads; war will spread everywhere, bringing down upon the world incommensurable devastation. (1993, #489)

It is perhaps relevant that 1993, the year in which this message was uttered, and 1994 were marked by the horrible civil wars in Bosnia, Rwanda and Chechnya as well as the continuing spread of AIDS.

Baptism of fire

Later the same year, Father Gobbi reminded a Japanese audience of the messages given at Akita, about fire falling from heaven.[41] He goes on to reiterate on his own (that is in the name of Mary):

Fire will come down from heaven and a great part of humanity will be destroyed. Those who will survive will envy the dead, because everywhere there will be desolation, death and ruin. (1993, #501)

In the message of October 13, 1994, Mary said, **"Fire will come down from heaven and humanity will be purified and completely renewed in such a way that it will be ready to receive the glorious Jesus who will return to you in glory."**[42] Taken by itself, this text might seem to be meant metaphorically; but in view of the messages of Akita, Garabandal and elsewhere,[43] it is probably to be taken literally.

---

[41] See the text above in chapter 1.

[42] From the message received during a retreat for priests preached at Effingham, Illinois (1994, #529).

[43] The texts from Garabandal and Akita were cited in chapter 1. Vassula also speaks of the Lord coming **"in flaming fire to extirpate from the earth and burn to the root all the evil of this world that is sunk in vice...."** (April 26, 1993; *True Life in God* VII, p. 10).

Mary's Heart our refuge

However, Mary's Immaculate Heart is **"The refuge, so sought for and awaited, for these times of the great trial which is now upon you"** (1993, #487). Moreover, we are given the assurance:

Statue of the Immaculate Heart of Mary carved in 1954 by Steiner; now in Sacred Heart crypt at the University of Notre Dame

The further you enter into the time of the great trial, the more will you experience, in an extraordinary way, my motherly presence close to you, to help, defend, protect and console you, and to prepare for you new days of serenity and peace. (1993, #486)

Mary herself will crush the head of the serpent, enchain the red dragon and defeat the Antichrist, **"in order to prepare the second coming of Jesus, who will restore His glorious reign among you"** (1990, #431). Likewise, Mary assures Father Gobbi that **"This most severe trial will be of short duration. Through my special intervention, these hours will be shortened"** (1975, #87). Elsewhere Mary adds that she needs our acts of reparation in order to shorten the great sufferings of these days (1993, #487).

The signs of the times

The time frame for the apocalyptic events is a topic to be approached with caution; Jesus told his disciples that it was not for them to know the day nor the hour of his return, but simply to be always ready for it. Mary likewise through Father Gobbi gives the following advice to priests:

There are even some who, in my name, believe that they can indicate the dates of events and exact occurrences, and they forget that the hour and the moment is a secret hidden in the merciful and fatherly heart of God.... And so I say to you, beloved sons, do not scrutinize the future...live only in the present instant, in complete abandonment close to my Immaculate Heart... (1975, #81m)

On the other hand, Jesus gave the apostles signs by which to know that his coming was near (Mt. 24:33). We have already noted that Father Gobbi insists that these signs are occurring now. Mary gave five specific signs to show that:

... the end of the times and the coming of Jesus in glory is very near... These signs are clearly indicated in the gospels, in the letters of Saint Peter and Saint Paul, and they are becoming a reality during these years.[44] The first sign is the spread of errors, which lead to the loss of faith and to apostasy.... The second sign is the outbreak of wars and fratricidal struggles... While natural catastrophes, such as epidemics, famines, floods and earthquakes, become more and more frequent.... The third sign is the bloody persecution of those who remain faithful to Jesus and to his gospel....

The fourth sign is the suppression of the true Eucharist, which we have already considered. **"The fifth sign consists in extraordinary phenomena which occur in the skies"** (1992, #485).

For Vassula, the great outpouring of the Holy Spirit in our times is, in a sense, the "sign of the Son of Man" spoken of in Mt. 24:30.[45]

---

[44] We saw references to St. Paul's Second Letter to the Thessalonian above. As for St. Peter, the allusion is probably to II Peter 3:5: "...in the last days, scoffers will come to scoff ... saying, `where is the promise of his coming? From the time when our ancestors fell asleep, everything has remained as it was from the beginning of creation.'"

[45] *True Life in God*, VII, p. 71 (Dec. 23, 1993). Farther on, Vassula explains that this refers to "a figurative sign before the visible sign in heaven" (p. 86; Apr. 12, 1994).

Father Gobbi, although he does not allude to this sign of the Son of Man, agrees that the Holy Spirit is especially active today:

> The Holy Spirit prepares hearts and souls for the second coming of Jesus. For this reason He is today pouring out his charisms in a manner which is even stronger and more extraordinary than at the time of the beginning of the Church, because you have now entered into the last times, which will lead you to the new Era.
>
> The task of the Spirit is to prepare humanity for its complete change, to renew the face of creation, to form the new heavens and the new earth. (1991, #450g)

How soon?

The visionaries of Garabandal and Medjugorje, as well as many others, have declared that the events they have predicted (the chastisement, as well as the warning and the sign that are to precede it) will take place "very soon." Even more precise indications have been given by others. After speaking apparently of a moment when the sky and all the elements will go up in flames, the Lord told Vassula, **"I will fulfil these prophecies in your own lifetime."**[46] (She was then 51 years old.) At Garabandal, it was promised that Joey Lomangino (a man blinded by an accident) will receive his sight back when the great miracle occurs; he is now in his 60's. Likewise, Conchita of Garabandal has been told that John Paul II will be the last pope (although it was specified that this refers to the end of an era, not the end of the world).[47]

From early on in his ministry, Father Gobbi has been making remarks such as **"The decisive events have begun"** (1975; 87) and **"My** [i.e. Mary's] **battle has now already begun"** (1977; 127). Nevertheless, in the last few years, he seems to insist much more that the last times are actually here. Above we saw his teaching that the great apostasy is already underway. In 1990 he said, **"The great trial has arrived for all humanity"** (437k). His messages for 1993 began with a similar statement (486s) and went on to say:

---

[46] *True Life in God*, VII, p. 69 (December 22, 1993).
[47] See chapter 1, p. xxx.

Now - as of this year - you have entered into the events which I foretold to you, and which are contained in the third part of the secret [of Fatima] which has not yet been revealed to you. This will now be made evident by the very events themselves which are about to take place in the Church and in the World" (489d).

In the fall of 1994, the message was given:

You have come to the culmination of the tribulation and you are living the years of the great chastisement which, in many ways, has already been announced to you. (August 28, 1994; #525)

Finally, Father Gobbi has stated expressly that "all" the Marian prophecies will come to fulfillment during the last decade of this century. In 1988 Mary requested:

... consecrate to me all the time that still separates you from the end of this century of yours.
It is a period of ten years. These are ten very important years. These are ten decisive years. I am asking you to spend them with me because you are entering into the final period of the second Advent, which will lead you to the triumph of my Immaculate Heart in the glorious coming of my Son Jesus.
In this period of ten years there will come to completion that fullness of time which was pointed out to you by me, beginning with La Salette all the way to my most recent and present apparitions.
In this period of ten years there will come to its culmination that purification which, for a number of years now, you have been living through and therefore the sufferings will become greater for all.
In this period of ten years, there will come to completion the time of the great tribulation, which has been foretold to you in Holy Scripture, before the second coming of Jesus.

In this period of ten years the mystery of iniquity, prepared for by the ever increasing spread of apostasy, will become manifest.

In this period of ten years all the secrets which I have revealed to some of my children will come to pass and all the events which have been foretold to you by me will take place. (1988, #389)

This text is a bit ambiguous about whether the ten years were to be counted from 1988 or from 1990, but several texts from 1990 indicate that the latter is the case:

During the last decade of your century, the events which I have foretold to you will have reached their completion (Jan 1, 1990, #417; similarly 419g and 428b).[48]

We saw above that 1998 was cited by Father Gobbi as the third multiple of 666, indicative of the time when Masonry will replace Christ and his Church with counterfeit human constructions (1989, #406). However, *he does not say that 1998 is the year in which this will happen*, but only that it indicates the "period of time" in which it will take place. (In the same vein, he took the year 666 to represent the rise of Islam and 1332 to symbolize the coming of a rationalistic mentality hostile to the faith; but neither of these were the precise dates of major events.)

The most exact indication comes in one of the most recently published messages:

...by the great jubilee of the year two thousand, there will take place the triumph of my Immaculate Heart, which I foretold to you at Fatima, and this will come to pass with the return of Jesus in glory, to establish his Reign in the world. Thus you will at last be able to see with your own eyes the new heavens and the new earth. (1994, #532)

---

[48] Father Gobbi himself confirmed, in a personal interview of October 11, 1994, that this is the correct interpretation of his previous texts.

This is an astonishing text. It affirms plainly that the triumph of Mary's Immaculate Heart will be accomplished by the year 2000. As if this were not surprising enough, it seems to imply that Jesus' return in glory will likewise take place by that date, because of the connection between the two events. This is somewhat confirmed by the promise that Father Gobbi himself will see the "new heavens and the new earth." We have seen an eloquent text about the latter in chapter 1; the present one suggests that they refer to the final kingdom that Jesus will establish on his return.

It is surprising to find Father Gobbi offering so precise a time limit for the coming of Christ. It is likewise difficult to imagine how so much could be accomplished in the few years that remain before 2000: the death of the Holy Father, the appearance of the Antichrist accompanied by the "horrible sacrilege," the chastisement, and finally the return of Christ to establish his Kingdom. Furthermore, there must be room for the conversion of Russia and the subsequent "period of peace" in the Fatima promises, to which Father Gobbi wholeheartedly subscribes.

There is perhaps a way to reduce this congestion somewhat. There are texts in which Father Gobbi (or Mary speaking through him) speaks of the "new Church of Light" that is now being formed *to prepare for* Christ's coming in glory:

> ... there is about to be born the new Church of Light, which my Son Jesus is forming for Himself in every part of the earth, so that it will be ready to receive Him with faith and with joy, in the proximate moment of His second coming. (1990, #435)

Similarly:

> Jesus is now forming this Church of His, by means of the powerful action of the Holy Spirit and in the Garden of the Immaculate Heart of your heavenly mother. It is the new Church of light, which has a splendor greater than a thousand suns put together.
> It is being formed in the hearts of the simple, of the little, of the pure, of the poor, of those who know how to receive and follow Jesus with perfect docility, with-

out any compromise with the spirit of the world. Jesus is building this, His new Church, in a way which is invisible and utterly mysterious: in silence, in hiddenness, in prayer, in simplicity, (1990, #429 cd; see also #428)[49]

Our texts speak of both a "new Church of Light" which will precede and prepare for the glorious return of Jesus, and a "new heavens and new earth" that will follow it. If the above reference to the triumph of Mary's Immaculate Heart (1994, #532) were to be understood as referring to the "new Church of Light," then it would not be necessary to postulate the return of Christ by the year 2000. In other words, her triumph would have a first phase in the "new Church of Light," and would be consummated in the "new heavens and new earth" when Christ returns at some later date. Admittedly, such a scenario does not fit the language of Father Gobbi quite so well as the other proposed above; however, it has the advantage of reducing somewhat the events to be compressed into the next few years, and it corresponds better with the Fatima promise that, after the consecration of Russia, "a time of peace will be granted to the world."[50]

Conclusion

However that may be, Father Gobbi warns us that we are living in a very serious time, which is why Mary is appearing in so many places and calling us so urgently to fast and pray. It is not merely because the world is in bad shape and needs repentance; we are entering into the last days of the world. The great apostasy, about which

---

[49] See also his texts on the Second Pentecost, e.g. 1990, 426, 428; on the new Church (1993, 496c).

[50] From the message of July 13, 1917. See, among other sources, *Lucia Speaks on the Message of Fatima* (Ave Maria Institute, Washington, N.J.) p. 31.

The scenario proposed here agrees likewise with that of Vassula, who teaches explicitly that fire of the Holy Spirit is going to purify the earth and make his home in us, transfiguring us into "His Holy City," in preparation for the return of Christ (*True Life in God*, vol. IV, pp. 154-155 [May 13, 1991]; cf. vol. VI, p. 58 [Oct. 5, 1992]). However, this is precisely one of the points of Vassula's teaching stigmatized as an "error" by a Notification of the Congregation for the Doctrine of the Faith of October 6, 1995.

Christ and St. Paul warned us, has already begun. For the present, the Holy Father is holding it back; but when he has been taken out of the way, the apostasy will become general under the reign of Antichrist. This terrible tribulation will be marked by the suppression of the Eucharistic sacrifice - either by an official ban, or at least by interpretations that empty it of its supernatural character. Mary's Immaculate Heart will be a shelter for her little ones during the reign of Antichrist, and their leader in the battle in which he will be overcome. After the world has been purified by a Baptism of Fire, the Age of the Holy Spirit will begin - a paradisiac state that will either prepare for or coincide with Christ's return in glory.

Such is the message of Father Gobbi. Will it prove to be only one more in the series of false apocalytic warnings that have emerged in history? Father Gobbi's depiction of and insights into the state of the Church today suggest that he is a man with a firm hold on reality. His personal holiness and fidelity to the Church, in contrast with the flamboyant egocentrism of so many TV evangelists, and likewise the fruitfulness of his ministry, inspire confidence in the messages that he claims to receive from Our Lady. Many particular points of his teaching are confirmed by other prophetic messengers of our time. All these factors indicate that he deserves to be taken seriously.

If that be so, what he says is not like a horror film which we can watch for the thrill of it. If the apostasy is under way now, we must either stand against it or yield to it. The chastisement, which most of us living today can expect to undergo, will be no trivial matter. Calling herself the "prophetess of these last times" (1991, #452), Mary summons us to be "apostles of the last times" (1991, #451). Our prayer and fasting can contribute, not only to our own salvation, but also to mitigating the chastisement and helping in the conversion of others. Mary does not say these things in order to terrify us, but to call us into the refuge of her Immaculate Heart. There we may not be preserved from suffering, but we will be protected from the influence of Satan and formed as a people ready to receive her Son.

– III –

THE IMPORTANCE OF APPARITIONS FOR THEOLOGIANS AND PASTORS

Neglect of Apparitions

Despite the prominence of apparitions in the life of the Church today, theologians and pastors have been reluctant to pay much attention to them. In the past, such things were usually treated in 'spiritual theology' under the heading 'extraordinary phenomena' of the mystical life. Since the Second World War, an impressive number of books and articles have been devoted to apparitions by authors of the stature of Yves Congar, Karl Rahner and Michel Labourdette. The centenary of Lourdes in 1958 evoked a little flurry of such studies, and René Laurentin[51] has pursued the topic intensively. The great majority of theologians, however (including Mariologists), seem not to give it serious attention.

Pastors

Some may suppose that such matters are properly the concern of those who have pastoral responsibility in the Church, rather than of theologians as such. However, most pastors - i.e. primarily bishops - are likewise very chary of taking a stand on such phenomena when these are reported in their dioceses. When compelled to make an investigation, they are likely, even in the face of overwhelming evidence, to retreat into the non-committal, *Non constat de supernaturalitate* ("The supernatural character of this event has not been established")[52] (I am not of course suggesting that whenever

---

[51] Besides those works of his listed in the bibliography, there is the immense research he has done on Lourdes and other particular apparitions.

[52] This is the standard canonical expression for declaring that the supernatural character of the event in question has not yet been proven beyond all doubt. It does not imply a positive *denial* of the supernatural character, although the newspapers sometimes treat it as if it carried such an implication.

this stand is taken, it is unjustified.) And ordinary priests, as experience abundantly shows, tend to react with skepticism and derision to reports of such things. In his book, *Visions and Revelations in the Spiritual Life*, Father Gabriel of St. Mary Magdalene constantly proposes as an example a devout little *philothea* who mainly needs to be directed away from the visions to which she is attached.[53] The disdainful tone he adopts is typical of Catholic clergy today.[54]

The disinterest of pastors is all the more striking in view of the fact that the impact of these apparitions on the people seems to be

greater now than ever before. Lourdes has a feast celebrated in the universal Church. Fatima has engendered the Blue Army plus innumerable smaller echoes. The Marian locutions re-ceived by Father Gobbi have led to the formation of the world-wide Marian

Medjugorje Conference at Notre Dame, 1995

Union of Priests, now embracing tens of thousands of members. Medjugorje has, in just twelve years, become a pilgrimage center with a universal appeal rivalling that of Lourdes or Guadalupe. The Medugorje conferences have become some of the biggest religious events in the United States and elsewhere. For five years in a row, the National Conference at the University of Notre Dame has drawn between 5,000 and 8,000 people, and dozens of regional and local conferences (some of them larger than Notre Dame's) have sprung up elsewhere. In response to the Medjugorje messages, people who never had engaged in such religious practices before

---

[53] Gabriel of St. Mary Magdalene, O.C.D. (1940) passim.

[54] I don't mean to suggest that this attitude is confined to our day. Mary of Agreda, writing in 1655, observes (without any tone of reproach) that in her day, "even prudent and wise persons, full of holy zeal in the spiritual life, are disturbed and troubled at the least mention of a higher life, looking upon visions and revelations as most suspicious and dangerous paths for the pursuit of Christian perfection." *City of God*, Introducton, #1 (tr. by "Fiscar Marison" [i.e. Rev. Geo. J. Blatter], So. Chicago, 1914).

are now praying the rosary daily (even the complete rosary) and fasting on bread and water. In Italy, a new religious community, Oasi *della pace,* has been inspired by Medjugorje. In Austria, a monthly journal of high quality - *Medjugorje Gebetsaktion* is devoted to Medjugorje, to say nothing of the innumerable newsletters and other publications appearing elsewhere.

In spite of this popular impact, apparitions have barely registered in the consciousness of most theologians and pastors. In the words of a modern commentator, "Although the apparitions have entered into the life of the Church, they do not yet seem to have entered into her thought."[55]

Part of the reason may be that the problem of apparitions, as it presents itself today, is unprecedented in the history of the Church. Although, to the best of my knowledge, we do not have available yet any serious history of Marian apparitions, or of apparitions in general,[56] still we are sufficiently informed to make some general observations.

The First Eleven Centuries

During the first eleven centuries, visions and apparitions were often reported in the lives of the saints, but it is very difficult to judge of their historicity, and in any case they do not seem to have had great importance or to have posed any serious problems. The earliest surviving reference to a Marian apparition appears in the life of St. Gregory Thaumaturgus (ca. 213-ca. 270), composed by St. Gregory of Nyssa (ca. 330 - ca. 395), grandson of St. Macrina, who had been instructed by the earlier Gregory.[57] According to this account, the elder Gregory, having reluctantly accepted the office of first bishop of Neocaesarea, prayed to God for light to guide him in this difficult ministry. The evangelist St. John subsequently appeared to him, accompanied by the Virgin Mary. The latter exhorted John to instruct Gregory in the mysteries of the faith, which John did, giving him a primitive but faithful formulation of the Trinitarian doctrine which is still extant.

---

[55] Louis Lochet (1960) p. 28.

[56] The fullest studies thus far are those of Volken (1963) and Adnès (1993).

[57] Migne, P.G. 46, 893-958.

Other famous examples include: Mary's appearance to St. James as he carried on his apostolate at Saragossa in Spain; "Our Lady of the Snows" indicating by a miraculous snowfall in August the place where a church was to be built in her honor (the future Santa Maria Maggiore); to Theophilus, who had made a written pact with the devil, and received it back through Mary's intervention so he could burn it; to St. John Damascene, restoring his severed hand; to the British Abbot Helsin saved at sea, with the request that he promote the feast of her Conception.[58] Whether rooted in historical fact or purely legendary, these stories served for the edification of those who heard them, but they were not the matter of pastoral, much less theological concern.

The High Middle Ages

In the high middle ages there is a rich outburst of visions and apparitions, chiefly to women. About them we are much more reliably informed through accounts composed either by the visionaries themselves or by people who knew them well. Although there are earlier precedents, the main stream can be said to have begun in the twelfth century with Hildegard of Bingen (1098-1179) and Elizabeth of Schönau (d. 1213), and to have flourished especially from the thirteenth to the fifteenth centuries. A few of the more famous are Angela of Foligno (1248-1309), Gertrude the Great (1255-c. 1302)

St. Simon Stock receiving the Scapular

and her sisters at Helfta, Hadewich (13th C.), Bridget of Sweden (1303-1373), Julian of Norwich (c. 1342-c.1413), Catherine of

---

[58] A detailed report on the early mediaeval apparitions is given by P. Mario Martins, S.J., "Narrativas de Aparições Marianas Até ao Séc XII," in *Maria et Ecclesia* XII (Roma, Pont. Acad. Mariana Internationalis) 77-111. Regrettably, I have not been able to read it because of the language.

Siena (1347?-1380), Frances of Rome (1384- 1440), Joan of Arc (1412-1431), and Catherine of Genoa (1447-1510).[59]

Mary appeared to some of these visionaries, but a scholarly review of the whole series suggests that visions of her were not particularly prominent.[60] On the other hand, three Marian apparitions during this period which had an immense effect on popular piety did not occur to any of the 'habitual' visionaries, but were attributed to three men not otherwise renowned for visions: St. Dominic (1170-1221), to whom the preaching of the rosary was said to have been confided; St. Simon Stock (c. 1247) to whom the scapular promise was given; and the Aztec Indian, Juan Diego (1474-1548). (One might also associate with them Mary's apparitions in 1233 and 1240 to the seven holy Florentines, leading to the foundation of the Servite Order.) Historical research has demonstrated conclusively that the rosary did not originate with St. Dominic, although the legend does well symbolize the role of the Dominicans in spreading this devotion.

Juan Diego's Tilma

The apparition to Simon Stock has not been refuted by historical research although, for want of documentation, we have little accurate information about it. Written records about Juan Diego are

---

[59] Many other less famous visionaries are listed by Adnès (1993), col. 980-981. It should be noted likewise that the line of mystics who are graced with visions and locutions in their personal lives would appear to continue to the present day in such figures as Mary of Agreda (1602-1665), Anne Catherine Emmerick (1774-1824), Padre Pio (1887-1968), Yvonne-Aimée de Malestroit (1901-1951), Marthe Robin (1902-1981), Gabrielle Bossis (d. 1950), and Alexandrina da Costa (1904-1955) - to give only a few random examples and without pretending to make a definitive judgment of their authenticity.

[60] Adnès (1993, col. 972-974), in listing the "characteristic types" of visions for this period, does not even mention Mary.

also late; but in his case there is the incomparable testimony of Mary's image left on his tilma.

St. Bridget and Gerson

St. Bridget of Sweden, perhaps the greatest and most influential visionary of all time, and surely one of the best documented, pro-

IOHANNES GERSON
THEOLOGUS, UNIVERSITATIS
PARISIENSIS CANCELLARI, ORATOR
ET LEGATUS REGIUS AD CONCILIUM
CONSTANTIENSE.
Optime in Concilio meritus, obiit in exilio 1429

vides also the classic case of a visionary being disregarded by a theologian - in this case, Jean Gerson (1363-1429), formerly chancellor of the University of Paris, perhaps the premier theologian of his day and the first in history to compose a systematic treatise on the discernment of spirits.[61] Throughout the greater part of Bridget's life, both Jesus and Mary appeared and spoke to her. She was given insights into the souls of those around her, visions of events in the life of Jesus, and premonitions of things to come. She was entrusted with messages for popes and kings, as well as for the people of her household. Ordinarily her revelations were concerned with very concrete and practical matters (such as the return of the Holy See from Avignon to Rome, in which, however, her efforts had to be completed by those of Catherine of Siena).[62]

Her canonization (in 1391, less than twenty years after her death), having been challenged, was reconsidered and confirmed

---

[61] Paschal Boland, O.S., *The Concept of* Discretio Spiritum *in John Gerson's* "De Probatione Spirituum" *and* "De Distinctione Verarum Visionum a Falsis" (Washington, Catholic University, 1959) p. 146. I have consulted this work, but have made my own translation of the texts cited below.

[62] The original seven books of Bridget's *Revelationes*, plus an eighth supplementary volume, were first printed by B. Gothan in Lübeck in 1492, and have been reprinted many times since then. A rich and helpfully organized selection of the more important revelations can be found in the English translation of Johannes Jorgensen's biography, *St. Bridget of Sweden* (London, Longmans, 1954).

by the Council of Constance (1414-1418). On this occasion Gerson, who had already composed a little treatise on the discernment of visions,[63] wrote another, "On testing the spirits."[64]

After introducing his topic, he says:

> ... this sacred Council seeks to deal with the canonization of saints and the examination of their teachings, especially those of one Bridget, who is used to receiving heavenly (*divinitus*) visions, not only of angels, but of Christ, Mary, Agnes and other saints, according to her claim. They maintain a perpetual familiarity with her, the way a spouse speaks to his spouse.[65]

Gerson goes on to point out that either to approve or disapprove such writings would have its danger:

> For what would be more unworthy of this Sacred Council, or alien to its function, than to give approval to false, imaginary or silly visions as if they were true and reliable revelations? But if it were now to denounce (*reprobare*) those visions which, in various countries, have been represented in many different ways and at many different levels as having received approval, there are serious grounds for fearing scandals in the Christian religion and in the devotion of the people. Even to maintain silence or let the issue lie would not, we fear, be without a certain element of danger now that the matter has come to public attention."[66]

Gerson himself is certainly open to the possibility of private revelations. His earlier treatise had alluded to "the attempts made by deceitful angels of undermine the authority of true miracles and the revelations of saints through sham works and magicians' tricks."[67] It likewise denounced the "sacrilegious impiety and in-

---

[63] Jean Gerson (1401).

[64] Jean Gerson (1415).

[65] Gerson 1415, *De Probatione Spirituum* (Glorieux ed. #5; Boland transl. #11).

[66] Ibid. Boland #12, 13.

[67] *De Distinctione Verarum Visionum a Falsis* (1401; Glorieux ed., p. 37. Boland transl. #7.)

credulity" of one who "rejects, denies and despises" such things as revelations.[68] A few years later, when Joan of Arc claimed to have been visited by angels and saints, Gerson would be one of the first to write favorably of her.[69]

But in regard to St. Bridget, while he does not formally take a position, the way in which he summarizes her claims (above) seems to invite skepticism. This impression is reinforced when Gerson makes the observation a few pages later that the fervor of women "is extravagant, overeager, changeable, uninhibited and therefore not to be considered trustworthy",[70] and that "it would be burdensome, not to say useless (*vanum*), to have to accept an immensity of visions upon visions as coming from the mouth of God and, therefore, to be believed with absolute faith".[71]

In a later work, *De examinatione doctrinarum*, which begins with the text, "Beware of false prophets," Gerson warned[72] against giving approval lightly to the visions of ignoramuses and uneducated little women ("*idiotas ac sine litteris mulierculas*"), declaring that Pope Gregory XI on his deathbed had cautioned against listening to those (men or women) who, under the guise of piety ("*sub specie religionis*") give utterance to the visions of their own heads. Gerson claims,[73] that this pope (who had returned the papacy from Avignon to Rome under the influence of Bridget, Catherine of Siena and Peter of Aragon) acknowledged having been misled by such people, thereby bringing the Church to the brink of schism (which schism actually occurred a few months after the Pope's death in 1378). Thus, in his attitude toward Bridget, and despite his avowed intention of steering a middle course between skepticism and credulity,[74] Gerson is a classic example of the theologian's disdain for visionaries.

Gerson's reservations did not deter Pope Boniface IX from canonizing Bridget in 1391, nor Martin V from confirming this

---

[68] Ibid.; Boland #10.

[69] Jean Gerson (1429).

[70] *De Probatione Spirituum* #7, p. 180 (Boland #22).

[71] Ibid. 8, p. 181 (Boland #28).

[72] J. Gerson (1423) p. 469.

[73] Gerson's testimony on this matter is, however, convincingly contradicted by Natalis Alexander, cited by the Bollandist editor of the article on St. Bridget in the *Acta Sanctorum*, vol. 52, p. 416, par. 199.

[74] On this, see the opening paragraph of *De Examinatione Doctrinarum*.

canonization in 1419 after it had been challenged. Pope Martin went on to declare that:

> ... this widow, by the grace of the Holy Spirit, merited the power of communicating to many the knowledge she had of their private thoughts, their intimate affections, their most secret attitudes; of hearing and seeing numerous revelations; and by the spirit of prophecy of predicting many things, some of which have in fact been fulfilled. These and other things besides are fully recounted in the book of her R*evelations*.[75]

After Gerson

Nevertheless, attacks on Bridget persisted. A group of critics culled 123 passages from her writings which they declared objectionable. In response, the Council of Basel (1431-1449) commissioned three theologians to examine them. The main result was a spirited defense of Bridget's work by one of the examiners, Juan de Turrecremata[76] (not to be confused with his more famous nephew, the Grand Inquisitor). Three centuries later, Cardinal Lambertini (later Benedict XIV), in his classic work on canonization, cited the revelations of St. Bridget as an example of "private revelations which are approved by the Apostolic See."[77] Thus Bridget, whose revelations and apparitions were among the earliest ever to be discussed by a major theologian, is also perhaps the one most solemnly approved by Church authority. (There is an interesting parallel two centuries later when Maria of Agreda is assailed by the theologian Eusebius Amort.)

Modern Marian Apparitions

Due allowance being made for the instances cited above, it is in the nineteenth century that the great Marian apparitions begin to occur

---

[75] *Acta Sanctorum*, October, vol. 4, p. 470. Cf. J. Fontanino, *Codex Constitutionum quas Summi Pontifices Ediderunt in Solemni Canonizatione Sanctorum* (Romae, 1729), p. 156.

[76] Juan de Turrecremata (1435).

[77] Benedict XIV (1734), Lib. III, cap. 53, n. 15.

and to take on an unprecedented role in popular piety. It should be noted that the term *apparition* is generally accepted as being a narrower term than *vision*. In the traditional classification of visions as either sensible, imaginary or intellectual, *apparition* would refer to a sensible vision, i.e. something seen with the bodily eyes, whereas *vision* used without qualification would be imaginary or intellectual, but not sensible. When the seers of Medjugorje insist that they see Mary in the same way that they see other people standing around, that her hair and her gown ripple in the same breeze that blows over the visionaries; that they even touch her, embrace and kiss her, they are describing an apparition. A dream, on the other hand, is not an apparition; nor is any other vision that takes place in the imagination, such as visions of past events, e.g. the scenes from the life of Christ seen by St. Bridget of Sweden or Mary of Agreda. Perhaps the line between apparitions and imaginary visions is not always hard and fast; and certainly there have been many phenomena which the records do not allow us to classify with certainty as one or the other. In any case, it is apparitions of the Blessed Virgin that have taken on an unprecedented importance in the life of the Church during the past two centuries, as we saw in chapter 1.

Marian Apparitions by Century

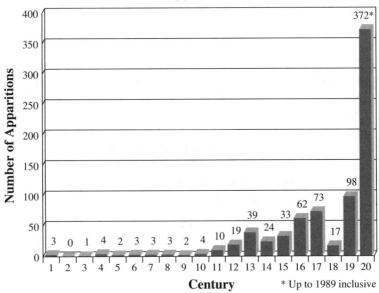

MARIAN APPARITIONS BY CENTURY

The accompanying graph is based on Robert Ernst's Lexikon der Marienerscheinungen (1989). This work is an attempt to list all the seriously attested Marian apparitions (together with visions and such phenomena as weeping and bleeding images) since the beginning of the Church. It would of course be impossible, as the author himself notes, to find records of literally all the apparitions that have occurred. It is also difficult in many cases to distinguish the genuine from the legendary; therefore he has restricted his list to events for which it is possible to determine the place and the date of the apparition, as well as the name of the person involved in it. Despite such precautions, the author has been historically very uncritical,* and inaccurate even in reporting contemporary phenomena.† Nevertheless, the work is a useful tool, and its statistics, even if imprecise, give an instructive indication about the relative frequency of reported apparitions over the centuries.

However, it should be noted that the contrast between the first and second millenia is probably exaggerated, first of all, because we are better informed about modern times than about the ancient. Secondly, Ernst's policy of taking no account of apparitions for which person, date and place cannot be determined eliminates from consideration many apparition stories widely circulated during the Middle Ages and which, whether legendary or true, were in the atmosphere.

That being granted, it would still appear that reports of Mary's interventions began to multiply significantly during the tenth century, and have continued to do so ever since (there was, however, a slight decline in the fourteenth century - the age of incipient "rationalism," and a great decline during the eighteenth - the time of the Enlightenment). The apparent drop in apparitions during the second century appears less anomalous if we bear in mind that those attributed to the first century are almost certainly the product of later legends.

According to this tabulation, the number of apparitions reported during the twentieth century alone is almost equal to the total number (400) from all the preceding centuries. When we bear in mind that there was still a decade of the century remaining when Ernst made his count, and that an immense number of apparitions not noted by him are occurring at present, an immense number, it seems sure that twentieth century will far surpass the total from the preceding centuries.

---

* He includes as historical, for example, the apparitions of Mary to the twelve apostles three days after the Assumption, and those at Saragossa in 41 A.D. and Le Puy in 47 A.D. In the present century, Necedah and Bayside make the list.

† In reporting the weeping Madonna of St. John of God Church in Chicago (explained in the *Illustrations credits* above), he speaks of the "cathedral of St. John of God," and adds that "Cardinal Joseph Bernardin of Chicago comes daily to reverence the statue."

Fear of Delusion

That is surely time enough for theologians and pastors to have given them serious thought. Why then have they been so reluctant to deal with this matter? The apostles gave the example by scoffing at the women from the tomb,[78] and priests have been following their example ever since. Fear of fraud or delusion is undoubtedly one of the basic reasons. This is the note that runs through Gerson's admonitions. Any priest experienced in pastoral ministry is likely to have encountered people with imaginary mystical experiences. Many a pastor is beset by a parishioner who claims to be receiving directives from the Lord as to how he should conduct his parish. Some people, as soon as they begin to experience graces of prayer, excitedly imagine that they have undergone extraordinary mystical phenomena; St. John of the Cross wrote some of his most trenchant lines on this subject. Consequently, many priests, like Father Peyramale at Lourdes or Father Aladel, the director of St. Catherine Labouré, are quite skeptical at the first report of apparitions.

But it is one thing to be cautious, quite another to be closed. Confronted with a reported apparition, it is a priest's duty to investigate, to test the spirits, to exercise discernment; if the case calls for caution, it demands also a fundamental openness to the possibility of divine intervention. Even if only rare exceptions prove to be genuine (something not lightly to be taken for granted), those exceptions are precious jewels that ought not be imperilled by being treated like trash. Some spiritual directors, in the style of Gerson, justify their coldness with the argument that if the thing is of God, it will survive harsh treatment, which will thus serve as a good test. They forget that visionaries are people too, and that for a person earnestly seeking to do God's will to be rebuked or scoffed at by a priest is cruel torture. When the Abbé Aladel dismissed Catherine Labouré's reports as delusions, his inconsiderateness and insensitivity brought Catherine intense anguish. On one occasion, the confessional in which she was speaking to him shook from her trembling.[79]

---

[78] I am indebted to Father John Mary Foster, C.S.J., for calling attention to this point.

[79] Cf. R. Laurentin, *Vie de Catherine Labouré* (Paris, Desclée de Brouwer, 1980), p. 137.

When episcopal committees blandly ignore serious evidence of the supernatural, they can be a source of scandal to little ones, who sometimes have eyes to see what is hidden from the wise and the learned. This is all the more so if the investigating committee does not do its work seriously, e.g. does not bother to interview all of the major witnesses, or ridicules the testimony presented. A pastor who had been closely involved in one of the more important modern apparitions told me that the diocesan committee conducting the investigation had declined to interview him, on the pretext that, since the parish boundary had been redrawn, he was no longer pastor of the apparition site.

Modern Skepticism

The caution that is naturally called for when there is question of supernatural phenomena is often reinforced and hardened by a second factor, an attitude which is the fruit of the Reformation and the Renaissance more than of Christian prudence. In rejecting the role played by the saints in Catholic piety, the reformers were led to scoff at the miraculous works and supernatural experiences attributed to the saints. Emphasis on faith alone impelled the Reformers to set aside 'signs' as detracting from the purity of faith. The renaissance, meanwhile, taught people to despise the "Middle Ages" as a barbarous trough between ancient and modern culture. Moreover, its critical studies exposed the legendary character of some of the mediaeval accounts, thereby evoking a skepticism that was too readily extended to all. Thus for very different motives, the Renaissance and Reformation combined forces in encouraging people to disregard 'mediaeval' miracles and apparitions. And once habituated to scoff at the stories of the past, they were predisposed to ignore those of the present.

When the Renaissance turned into the Enlightenment, this skepticism was reinforced by a new confidence that Reason is adequate to discover any truth. In a still cruder form, there was a naive confidence in the ability of science to attain all that was knowable and to explain all that takes place. In such a rationalistic and scientist atmosphere, when even the existence of God and the immortality of the soul began to be denied, preternatural phenomena were simply disregarded without examination. Although today's culture is beginning to realize the sterility and inadequacy of this extreme rationalism and reliance on science, we are still heavily influenced by it.

Psychologists

Many of the psychological systems arising out of this rationalistic mentality have inherited its skepticism towards "the supernatural." The works of grace and the free initiatives of the Creator are matters beyond the competence of any human discipline; but this has not hindered psychologists, especially pop- psychologists, from arrogating to themselves the role of investigating and passing judgment on all that takes place in the human soul. No doubt there are also psychologists who, though working from a purely naturalistic and rationalistic point of view, have felt obliged to make room for the `paranormal' - a heterogeneous grab-bag in which preternatural phenomena along with other experiences of a totally different nature might be comprised. This is very interesting and worthy of serious consideration; nevertheless, the overall impact of modern psychology has been to persuade its disciples that all so-called mystical or supernatural (and perhaps even spiritual) phenomena are susceptible of a natural and physical explanation. Even some priests and theologians have been influenced by such an attitude, which amounts to a surrender of the rights of their own faith-inspired discipline to the arrogant pretensions of those who are oblivious to the limits of the psychological disciplines.

Thus the priest-psychiatrist, Marc Oraison, in presenting what he calls "the clinical psychiatric physician's point of view,"[80] interprets all apparitions, even those of Lourdes and Fatima, as hallucinations. He condescendingly grants that the recipients may be sincere, but with serene confidence explains that "the subconscious of the subject expresses itself in using visual symbols to express its deep desire" (p. 138). In a mirage, a man dying of thirst in the desert imagines he sees water because he so badly wants to. Oraison pronounces the case of apparitions to be similar, only more complex (involving the whole cultural, emotional and familial conditioning of the subconscious - p. 139).

---

[80] M. Oraison (1976) (pp. 127-151).

The danger of hallucination was well recognized by spiritual writers long before the age of psychiatry. What is 'new' in the psychiatric explanation, besides its invocation of the subconscious, is the assurance with which the possibility of a real apparition is simply disregarded. Despite the complexity and difficulty of the matter, which Oraison acknowledges, and while insisting on the need of scientific attitudes and methods, he does not hesitate to declare what the result of a "profound study of the subject" would produce -even without having undertaken to make such a study.

The Place of Apparitions in Christianity

But radical skepticism about apparitions is irreconcilable with the fundamental place they hold in the Christian religion. Theophanies and other preternatural manifestations of the divine were already familiar in the Old Testament. God is often said to

God speaks to Moses
(Steffen Arndes, *Bible*, Lübeck, 1499)

have appeared or to have spoken to Adam, Noah, Abraham, Isaac, Jacob and others. He manifested himself in Jacob's ladder, in the

Fresco of the Annunciation,
Marytown (Libertyville, IL)

Burning Bush, at Mt. Sinai and in the column of fiery cloud which led the Israelites through the desert and shielded them from the Egyptians. Visions played a great role in the ministry of Daniel, Ezekiel and other prophets. There were apparitions of angels to Abraham

From the Book of Hours *of Jean, Duke of Berry*

and Jacob, and angel stories in the books of Tobit, Daniel and others. The dead Samuel manifested himself in response to the witch of Endor (I Sam. 28:7-20).

It is in the New Testament that apparitions in particular take on their full role. Christianity began with the apparition of the angel Gabriel to Mary (to say nothing of his previous appearance to Zech-ariah). Moses and Elijah appeared to Jesus at the Transfiguration; Satan showed himself to Jesus in the desert; angels ministered to him there as well as in the Garden of Olives.

The faith of the Church is based on the apparitions of the risen Lord to the disciples. (We may sometimes forget that all of the manifestations of the glorified Jesus were apparitions in the strict sense.[81])

After the Ascension, apparitions, visions and locutions of various sorts continued to sustain the primitive Church. The manifestations of the Holy Spirit in the form of a dove and of tongues of fire were a kind of apparition. Jesus appeared to Stephen at his martyrdom (Acts 7: 55) and also to St Paul, once to convert him (Acts 9) and later to declare that he

St. John sees the woman clothed with the sun. (Woodcut by Johannes Otmar in *Plenarium,* Reutlinger, 1482)

would have to bear witness in Rome (Acts 23:11).[82] Angels appeared to the apostles (Acts 5:19), to Peter in particular (Acts 12:7), to Cornelius (Acts 10:3), and apparently to Philip (Acts 8:26).

---

[81] The term *apparition* does not imply that Jesus' real body was not involved, but simply that, while in the state of glory, he made himself present to the disciples there where he was not naturally present. Many of Mary's apparitions today are similar: the visionaries can touch and embrace her, they see her hair and her dress waving in the same earthly wind that is blowing on them. *Apparition* is not to be equated with a *vision*, which takes place in the mind or imagination of the seer.

[82] Perhaps also when sending him to Jerusalem (cf. Gal. 2:2).

Peter's vision of the sheet let down from heaven instructed him to welcome the gentiles (Acts 10:9-16). Paul likewise had a vision of a Macedonian calling him to come and evangelize (Acts 16:9). The last book of the New Testament is a long series of visions and/or apparitions. It would therefore appear that St. Peter was articulating a kind of basic statute of the Christian regime when, on Pentecost Day, he told his listeners that they were witnessing the fulfillment of the prophecy of Joel, "Your young men shall see visions, your old men shall dream dreams" (Acts 2:17). From all this, we can conclude that apparitions and visions played a fundamental role in the establishment of Christianity by Jesus, and continued to play a significant role in the life of the primitive Church.[83]

The conversion of St. Paul

This would suggest that these things are a normal part of Church life. As Bishop Pio Bello Ricardo declared, in affirming the authenticity of the apparitions at Betania:

> Apparitions and visions can be referred to as constants in the history of salvation.... From the Church's patristic origins to our days there have been numerous apparitions which have been turning points in the history of the Church. These apparitions form part of the charismatic dimension of the Church, which is associated with its ministerial dimension (though we must note that the ministerial dimension is a charism in itself).[84]

---

[83] A much more complete list of the apparitions and visions of both New and Old Testaments is given by Cardinal Lambertini, subsequently Pope Benedict XIV, in *Doctrina de Servorum Dei Beatificatione et Beatorum Canonizatione*, Lib. III, cap. 50. As for those that have occurred in the history of the Church, he refers (n. 7) to Martin Delrio S.J. (1551-1608) and Domenico Gravina O.P. (1574-1643) who have treated this matter at great length.

[84] Cited from *The Bridge to Heaven* by Drew Mariani and Michael Brown (Marian Communications, POB 8, Lima PA, 19037), p. 147. (I have slightly altered the clumsy English translation given there.)

Hence, when apparitions are reported today, they deserve to be considered cautiously but seriously, like anything pertaining to the order of grace. In fact, however, despite the papal approbations of St. Bridget, it is Gerson's skeptical attitude that has prevailed among pastors and theologians of our time.

Can Theology Ignore Charisms?

Even when willing to acknowledge the genuineness of contemporary apparitions, some theologians would maintain that these things do not concern them. Since Jesus has already given us all that is necessary for salvation, they argue, we are not dependent on the truth of any new revelations. Although valid enough if rightly understood, this principle has been over-emphasized and understood rigidly and one-sidedly, due to failure to take into consideration a complementary truth, namely, that God continues to act among his people day by day. In founding the Church, Jesus did indeed give it everything necessary in terms of doctrine and sacraments; but he did not make it self-sufficient. It depends on his help from moment to moment, and without it would collapse.

Jesus' On-going Action in the Church

He promised that he would remain with us until the end of time and give his Spirit to teach and inspire us. This promise cannot be restricted to the ordinary graces that are received through the sacraments and prayer; it also includes the charismatic figures that God raises up from time to time to revivify the faith of his people. Saints Bernard, Peter Damian, Francis of Assisi, Dominic, Vincent Ferrer, Bernardine of Siena, Anthony of Padua, Catherine of Siena, Joan of Arc and Ignatius Loyola are just a few random examples. One may suspect that Padre Pio and Mother Teresa of Calcutta will likewise be recognized one day as among the great charismatics of our own time. But I say this, not in the abusive sense in which today anyone with a natural gift of eloquence or leadership is called charismatic. By *charism*, I mean an extraordinary gift given by God to an individual who is called to an exceptional ministry in the

Church. (I recognize that charism can also be understood as embracing ordinary gifts and graces, but these are not pertinent here.)

The most important charism is prophecy (cf. I Cor. 14:1-5), which is not primarily prediction but being charged with a message for God's people. "You must go to everyone I send you to and say whatever I command you," God said in commissioning Jeremiah (Jer. 1:7). Although the appearance of a prophet in any particular situation is altogether unpredictable, the charism of prophecy is a normal, on-going function in the People of God. Amos in fact went so far as to declare, "The Lord God does nothing without revealing his secrets to

Joan of Arc

his servants, the prophets" (3:7). St. Paul laid down regulations for the use of prophecy as though it were a normal peice of equipment in the Christian community (I Cor. 12, 13 and especially 15). St. Thomas Aquinas, referring to the time after Christ, generalized the principle, "At each period, there were always some who had the spirit of prophecy..."[85]

Apparitions cp. Charisms

Apparitions are another way in which God's ongoing action and care for the Church are manifested. They are like charisms in being free and unpredictable ways, not bound up with any office, in which the Lord uses human means to provide for his people. When the apparition delivers a message to the Church, as was the case at Fatima, this is something resembling the charism of prophecy.

---

[85] St. Thomas Aquinas, *Summa Theologiae*, I-II, 174, 6 ad 3. The Potter translation which I have cited is a little bit free, but catches faithfully the sense of the original: "...singulis temporibus non defuerunt aliqui prophetiae spiritum habentes."

I would not go so far as to call apparitions an instance of prophecy, as does Laurentin,[86] or even speak of them as charisms without qualification. A charism is a spiritual gift empowering the recipient for some ministry in service of the Church. An apparition is not properly a gift, since it does not become the possession of the recipient; and it is not an empowerment. It is simply another way, sui *generis*, in which God manifests himself or his designs to mankind. Even when it entails a message, the apparition differs from prophecy. A prophet inspired to speak in the name of God does not normally receive a message already formulated, which he merely has to repeat; the prophet himself formulates the message he delivers. It is in his mind that the divine communication become expressed in human language. This is done under divine inspiration, and perhaps without the prophet himself understanding all the implications of his message; nevertheless it is the prophet who puts it into words. But when Mary gives a message to Juan Diego, Bernadette, Lucia, Melanie or any other visionary, it is Mary who formulates the message; the visionary's role is merely to repeat it. The visionaries are perhaps comparable, not to the prophets, but to the disciples of the prophets who repeated the teaching of their masters. (However, I don't mean to affirm a rigid distinction between prophet and visionary, but simply to indicate two poles, between which there may be intermediate positions. Even when the message is from Our Lord or the Blessed Mother, the language usually seems to be that of the visionary.)

Whatever be their precise distinction, apparitions like charisms are expressions of the Lord's on-going presence in and care for his Church. This is obvious when Jesus himself appears, as in the revelations of the Sacred Heart. Apparitions of the saints are indirectly a sign of the presence of Jesus; more directly, they exemplify the great truth of the Communion of saints. This is a basic article of faith, quite independently of apparitions; but the latter make it come alive for the believer.

Message of the Marian Apparitions

The most frequent apparitions are those of the Blessed Virgin. This accords with the doctrine of the Assumption: Mary alone, of all the

---

[86] Laurentin (1976), p. 164 ff.

saints, has a body in which to appear. (The bodies with which the other saints appear pose somewhat of a theological problem, since the bodies in which they walked the earth have perished.) Moreover Mary's coming is not merely one instance of the Communion of saints; it is specifically a reminder and illustration of her *spiritual maternity.* Nothing is more characteristic of a mother's role than to be present to her children, especially when they are in trouble. We saw in chapter 1 that the chief motivation of the modern apparitions seems to be that the human race is in a sinful condition which is calling down God's punishment. Mary of the recent apparitions stress the "chastisement" that is imminent.[87] Through Father Gobbi, Mary has said that the reason she is appearing so often today is to call us to conversion, penance and prayer in order to "shorten the hours of purification."

Basically, this message is nothing other than a renewal of the Gospel call to conversion, prayer and penance. The warning of an impending chastisement echoes the message of Jesus himself, as well as that of the prophets and apostles. The announcement of this punishment fo*r our time* goes beyond the letter of the New Testament, of course, and presumably would never be authenticated officially by the Church; but the application of the Gospel message to a particular time and place is precisely the role of post-biblical prophecy.[88]

The Structure of Theology

Another reason why some theologians leave apparitions out of consideration derives from their conception of Sacred Theology. The latter is understood to be concerned primarily with the canonical

---

[87] Besides La Salette in the last century, Garabandal, Medjugorje and Akita give particularly acute expressions to this theme which, moreover, is echoed in many other apparitions and messages of Our Lady.

[88] St. Thomas Aquinas says, in his treatise on prophecy, "In every age men have been instructed by God as to what they ought to do, according as it was expedient for the salvation of the elect" (*Summa Theologiae* II-II, 174, 6), adding, "there have never been lacking men with the spirit of prophecy, not it is true to develop a new doctrine of faith, but to direct human activity" (ibid., ad 3).

Revelation, that is to say, with the Gospel of Jesus Christ as communicated through his Apostles and interpreted by Sacred Tradition. In this view, the theologian's task is that of investigating Revelation, making it as intelligible as possible, drawing out its hidden implications, and applying it to modern life and culture. Since apparitions and the 'private' revelations associated with them, even if authentic, can never become incorporated into the canonical Revelation on which the Church is based, they would appear to be extraneous to Sacred Theology.

This conception of theology highlights the important principle that new revelations do not provide new theological principles comparable to those we have from Scripture and Sacred Tradition. But if taken to mean that the theologian has only to contemplate the truths revealed by Jesus in abstraction from all that is going on in the world today, such a conception of theology would not be widely accepted. And if theology has to task of confronting the eternal Gospel with the information, insights and configurations of contemporary society, surely any probable interventions of God in our world today belong to the matter that the theologian needs to scrutinize.

St. John of the Cross

The view that apparitions are a normal part of Church life can be objected to on the grounds that authorities on mystical and spiritual theology almost universally class them among the 'extraordinary phenomena' of mysticism,[89] but there is really no contradiction here. Spiritual writers usually focus on the life of an individual, in which apparitions are indeed extraordinary. No particular person has a right to expect them. To yearn for them or, when they actually occur, to be attached to them, would be to

---

[89] Cf. Gabriel of St. Mary Magdalen (1940), p. 34; Adolphe Tanquerey, *The Spiritual Life*, 2nd ed. (Tournai, Desclée, 1930) p. 701 ff.; Antonio Royo Marin, O.P., *The Theology of Christian Perfection*, (New York, Foundation for a Christian civilization) p. 578; and innumerable other modern manuals of spirituality.

the detriment of one's union with God. It is in this sense that the warnings of St. John of the Cross in The *Ascent of Mount Carmel* are to be understood:

> Under the ancient law prophets and priests sought from God revelations and visions which indeed they needed, for faith as yet had no firm foundation and the Gospel law had not yet been established.... But now that faith is rooted in Christ, and the law of the Gospel has been proclaimed in this time of grace... there is no need for any further revelation.... Therefore, anyone who wished to question God or to seek some new vision or revelation from him would commit an offense, for instead of focusing his eyes entirely on Christ he would be desiring something other than Christ, or beyond him.[90]

In reading this text, we need to bear in mind that John of the Cross himself was so favored with visions and revelations as to become the Church's chief authority on the subject. The danger against which he warns is not that of receiving such things, but of seeking them. That is not our problem. We are concerned with apparitions that occur without being sought for, that are due to God's initiative, not man's.

To disregard this sort of grace on the pretext that, having the Gospel, we don't need any further revelation, would be to adopt a posture like that of King Achaz. When invited by the Lord himself to ask for a sign, he piously answered, "I will not ask, I will not tempt the Lord!" For this he was severely rebuked, and the Lord went on in spite of him to accord the greatest sign ever given in salvation history: "the virgin shall be with child, and bear a son, and shall name him Immanuel" (Isaiah 7:10-14).

In the life of the Church, just as it is normal that there occasionally arise individuals endowed with the charisms of prophecy, healing etc., so also it is normal that there be apparitions and visions of Jesus, Mary and the saints.[91] By n*ormal,* I do not mean

---

[90] *The Ascent of Mount Carmel*, II, 22. See all of chapters 9-28.

[91] On this point, see the strong affirmation of John Arintero in *The Mystical Evolution in the Development and Vitality of the Church* (Herder 1951; republished by Tan Books in 1978), especially Part II, ch. 5, "Visions and Locutions."

there is a law whereby such things can be predicted, or that they will occur with any regularity. By their very essence, they are free interventions, and there is no telling when or where they will occur. When startled visionaries such as Ivan Dragicevic ask, "Why me?" they are never given a reason except that God is pleased to make use of instruments that appear unsuitable. But God has made it evident that it is in fact his will to let the saints, and above all his Blessed Mother, appear in the world from time to time to encourage us and to warn us, according to our needs.

Faith in Apparitions

An important question for our topic concerns the kind of faith that may be directed to apparitions. This question is usually posed in regard to 'private revelations' rather than apparitions as such; but much the same principles would seem to apply to both. There is no space here to review the history of this question, which has been complicated by use of the notion of "ecclesiastical" or "Catholic" faith as designating not merely the matter of faith (*fides quae*) but the specific modality of its act (*fides qua*). I suggest that it may be better to set aside this questionable notion, and consider separately two distinct questions: first, whether the faith given to private revelations and apparitions is supernatural (divine) or merely natural; and second, what the implications are of the approval given by the Church to a particular apparition. The first question can be reworded thus: is the belief accorded to a 'private revelation' an act of 'divine faith' -like the faith we have in Christ and in his teachings, or of mere human faith - such as we have in things that other people tell us? When the question is so put, theologians as different as John of St. Thomas, Suarez and Karl Rahner agree that private revelations (and presumably apparitions) can be the object of divine faith.[92]

---

[92] This view had largely been lost sight of in modern theology until Rahner renewed it in his own way. When the Congregation of Rites says, in the text of Pope Pius cited below, that "only human faith" is to be given to private revelations, I don't believe that this other view is being excluded. More likely it has just been overlooked in the effort to distinguish between what is a matter of Church doctrine and what is a matter of private belief.

The reason, as I see it, lies in the fact that an authentic apparition is ultimately a message from God addressed to human beings. God surely does not let them occur without an accompanying grace; hence the recipients have a certain obligation to recognize and assent to his action. (The obligation to accept a grace may or may not be under pain of sin.) Rejecting a genuine apparition today would not be essentially different from rejecting those of biblical times (e.g. Zechariah doubting the word of the angel Gabriel). Of course, it may well happen that some of the people who hear about an apparition do not receive the grace to believe in it; or they may encounter it in circumstances that effectively block their minds to it through no fault of their own. But this can happen also in the case of faith in Christ. There can be people who, in all sincerity, therefore without sin, fail to recognize explicitly that he is the Son of God; but that does not change the fact that those who receive the appropriate grace are bound to believe. By the same token, those to whom Our Lady appears, and to whom the grace to believe is given, are doing wrong if they fail to accept it. Modern apparitions, to be sure, are not equal in importance to those of the risen Christ on which our faith is founded; but as acts of God, they place essentially the same kind of demand on us. Due proportion guarded, therefore, those who refuse to believe, when offered the grace to do so, would seem to be guilty, if not of sin, at least of closing themselves to grace. (Isn't this what is suggested by St. Catherine Labouré when, on hearing about what was taking place at Lourdes, she remarked, "If only the superiors had been willing, those things could have taken place in our chapel"?)[93]

The faith of a visionary could be compared to that of the apostles who saw the risen Jesus with their own eyes, while the faith of people who merely hear about the vision could be compared to that of the disciples to whom the apostles preached. In both cases, the assent is a religious act because motivated, not merely by the human evidence perceived, but by the testimony of God within. "Blessed are you Simon, Son of Jonah. Flesh and blood have not revealed that to you, but my Father who is in heaven" (Mt. 16:17). God gave Peter the grace to recognize Jesus as the Messiah and Son of God. He likewise opened the heart of Lydia to believe in the

---

[93] René Laurentin, *Vie de Catherine Labouré* (Paris, Desclée de Brouwer), p. 148.

preaching of St. Paul (Acts 16:14). In the case of modern apparitions, it is to be presumed that God gives the grace to believe in the apparition both to the visionary and also to all those for whom the apparition is meant (maybe only a handful of people; maybe a great multitude). There is no apparent reason why the faith called for would not have the same character as faith in Christ, even though it is not of equal importance. And if the people to whom the vision is addressed refuse to believe, whereas they do believe in Christ, may they not be comparable to the pharisees and sadducees who believed in Moses and the prophets of old, but refused to acknowledge the Son of God standing before them?

I repeat, the two cases are not of equal gravity. Faith in an apparition is not essential to salvation as is faith in Jesus. All I am proposing is that it is a religious act of the same generic character, namely, an act of faith in God, invited and inspired by the grace of God. And just as we do not know who, among those who professedly reject Jesus, are really guilty of the sin of unbelief, with still greater reason we must withhold from judging those who do not believe in a given apparition (since ordinarily we do not even know if it is meant for them).

Church Approval of Apparitions

The second question posed above has to do with the implications of the approval which the Church has given to certain apparitions. What is sometimes called the 'classic' position was enunciated by the Congregation of Rites in 1877[94] and reiterated by Pius X in his encyclical against Modernism:

> In passing judgment on pious traditions, be it always
> borne in mind that in this matter the Church uses the great-
> est prudence, and that she does not allow traditions of

---

[94] *Decreta Authentica Congregationis Rituum*, t. III, 1900, n. 3419 (May 12, 1877). This text, responding to the enquiry of three bishops as to whether the Holy See had approved the apparitions of Lourdes and La Salette, repeats a response of February 6, 1875, to the Archbishop of Santiago, Chile, who had raised a similar question about an apparition Our Lady in Barcelona (Ibid. n. 3336).

Pope St. Pius X

this kind to be narrated in books except with the utmost caution and with the insertion of the declaration imposed by Urban VIII. Even then she does not guarantee the truth of the fact narrated; she simply does not forbid belief in things for which human arguments are not wanting. On this matter the Sacred Congregation of Rites, thirty years ago, decreed as follows: "These apparitions and revelations [of La Salette and Lourdes] have neither been approved nor condemned by the Holy See. It has simply allowed that they be devoutly believed by purely human faith, according to the tradition which they relate, corroborated by suitable testimonies and documents.[95]

Fifty years later, however, Carlo Balíç, O.F.M., proposed that Lourdes was an exceptional case, since "the ecclesiastical magisterium has given a clear, explicit and positive approval to the fact of Lourdes."[96] Pursuing this line of thought, F. Roy collected the various statements of the Church's approval of Lourdes, and concluded that the faithful were indeed under an obligation "to give to the fact of Lourdes an assent that is religious, interior, etc." (To characterize this assent, he invented the name, "ecclesial faith.")[97]

No doubt, it is the ordinary practice of the Church to refrain from judging the authenticity of a revelation or apparition and merely to declare it to be not in conflict with the teaching of Christ, as Pius X indicated. This is because the Revelation on which the Church is founded, and which it has the responsibility to guard, proclaim and interpret, is solely that imparted by Jesus through the apostles. New

---

[95] Pius X, *Acta Sanctae Sedis*, 40 (1907) 649. In the English translation in *Official Catholic Teachings*. *Christ Our Lord* (Wilmington, Consortium, 1978) this text comes towards the end of par. 164, on p. 119.

[96] C. Balíç (1958) p. 103.

[97] F. Roy (1962), p. 32.

revelations may well be given in any epoch, but never enter into the 'canonical' Revelation. However, nothing prohibits the Church from making a more positive appraisal. Revelations and apparitions are matters of great concern to her, because of their powerful influence on the life of the faithful. They call for discernment, so that the good and authentic can be separated from the false and harmful. And as Roy and others have argued, the approval given to certain apparitions, such as those of Paray-le-Monial, Lourdes and Fatima, would seem to go well beyond a mere permission to believe, and to imply a positive affirmation of their authenticity.

Whether this affirmation satisfies the criteria for infallibility is another question. Only a small part of Church teaching is proposed in such a manner as to guarantee its infallibility. Maintaining that the Church has given positive approval to these apparitions does not imply that it has employed the same degree of authority here as in dogmatic definitions. I would maintain that the Church has indeed approved certain apparitions in the sense of recognizing their authenticity, but would leave open the question whether this judgment is infallible.

The Concern of Pastors and Theologians

Now we are in a position to address our principal question - in what way do Marian apparitions concern the pastor and theologian? As regards pastors, the answer should be evident from what has been said thus far. Apparitions belong to the life of the Church as a sign of the ever-present assistance of the Holy Spirit and the Communion of saints. They are a powerful stimulus to the religious spirit of the faithful. When they are neglected, the Church suffers loss. By the same token, frauds or delusions do harm, especially when undetected. To discern between those that are authentic and those that are delusional, and in the authentic to discern further what is of God and what is of human origin, and finally to give direction about how to incorporate the apparitions healthily into one's spiritual life - these are all pastoral functions of the highest importance.

The case of theologians is a bit more complex. First of all, on the practical level, their expertise is useful to pastors for the task of discernment. Hence, for the common good of the Church, theologians ought to study reported apparitions seriously and bring what light they can to bear on them.

Even if we limit our consideration to the theologian's proper function as theologian, apparitions still ought to interest him. There is a prima fa*cie* incongruity in someone being devoted professionally to the theology of Mary while unconcerned about whether Mary herself is acting and appearing in our world. He would be rather like a liturgist who doesn't go to Mass.

If we seek to put a finger on the precise reason for this incongruity, it is not that apparitions may contribute something new to the subject matter of his discipline. As was noted above, the subject matter of theology is limited by the Word of God - in itself, and in all the implications that can be drawn from it. Neither are apparitions of any great weight as apologetic arguments. Although people are sometimes converted to the Church because of apparitions -this is an especially prominent feature at Medjugorje - the apparition does not seem to function as an argument so much as an occasion of grace.

As I see it, the proper reason for the theologian's concern is to be sought in the connection between theology and life. Christian theology needs to be rooted in Christian life; and the Marian apparitions pertain, as I have tried to show, to the 'vitality' of this life. That is to say, they are an important means by which the Holy Spirit touches the heart of the Christian people.

I am not implying that the quality of theology is proportional to the theologian's piety. Ever since the Middle Ages, the distinction has been recognized between two kinds of knowledge of God, one that comes from intimate personal contact with him - what is commonly called "the wisdom of the saints," and rational or systematic theology, which can be cultivated even by those who are not very devout, provided only they have faith. I do not challenge the validity of this distinction. But here, as in so any other areas, a distinction has been hardened into a separation, distorting its meaning. Rational, scientific theology is indeed distinct from the science of the saints, but it ought to be rooted in a life of holiness, and suffers if it is not.

Jesus himself said that divine wisdom has been hidden from the learned and clever, but revealed to little ones (Mt. 11:25). St.

Paul added that the wisdom of God is foolishness in the eyes of the world (cf. I Cor 1:18). Up until the scholastic period, nearly all the great theologians were in fact saints, the reason being not only that love of God is the normal motive for studying about God, but also that closeness to God gives a certain 'taste' or 'feel' for the things of God, thereby strengthening one's theological judgment. One who has only "book learning" lacks firm judgment about divine things. He may be well informed about Scripture and the teachings of the great theologians and philosophers; he may understand the logic of their arguments, but he will not have that sensitivity which comes only from closeness to God, or better, connaturality with the things of God.

If it be granted that theology should be rooted in piety, then Marian apparitions will be relevant to the theologian inasmuch as they pertain to piety. They are not indeed the chief source of the latter; they do not provide it with the substance that is to be found in the sacraments and sacred preaching. One can be a good and holy Christian while remaining unconvinced about many particular apparitions. Still the latter constitute one of the ways the Holy Spirit is nourishing the devotion of the Christian people today. Anyone who loves the Blessed Virgin will spontaneously be interested in what she is doing in the contemporary world. To disregard apparitions systematically, or to reject those particular ones which, in God's providence, have been offered to us, is to spurn a grace of God and thus to damage our personal relationship to him. This will naturally tend to maim our theology also.

One would expect that those who emphasize the role of personal experience in theology would be especially sensitive to this need. It is therefore somewhat incongruous that our age should be, on the contrary, one in which apparitions are little regarded by professional theologians.

It must not be overlooked that neither theologians nor pastors are exempt, any more than the laity, from that need of God's gracious help that makes apparitions useful and, in a real sense, necessary for the Church on its pilgrimage through time. Churchmen too are in need of encouragement, admonition and guidance in the struggle to maintain the Christian life in a world dominated by an alien spirit. If they have the advantage of being more learned about the Gospel message than the average person in the pews, they are also more subject to the snares of the Enemy. In particular, they are prone to a spiritual pride which turns the Christian reality into a mummy - brittle bones wrapped in a sack of dry skin which, even if it retains every bit of the body that once was, lacks the spirit without which there is no life.

Hence it is not surprising that the messages accompanying apparitions are sometimes directed expressly to the clergy. Father Gobbi's locutions are nearly all addressed through him to Mary's "beloved priests." Although usually deferential and imbued with reverence for the priestly office, the messages sometimes bemoan the failure of priests to live up to their role. Occasionally they contain stern admonitions. Our Lord gave Vassula a warning applicable to theologians as well as to pastors:

> ...the hour will come when men of power will enter My Sanctuary, men who do not come from Me; in fact this hour is already here; I, Jesus Christ, wish to warn My priests, bishops and cardinals, I wish to warn all My House of a great tribulation; My Church is approaching a great tribulation; remember, I have chosen you, by My sanctifying Spirit, to glorify Me; I have chosen you from the beginning to be the sturdy pillars of My Church and to live by faith in the Truth. I have chosen you to share my Glory and to shepherd My lambs; I tell you solemnly that you will soon be tested by fire; pray and fast so as not to be put to the test; stand firm and keep the traditions you were taught; obey My pope* no matter what comes up; remain faithful to him and I will give you the graces and the strength you will need; I urge you to keep faithful to him and keep away from anyone who rebels against him; ... soon you will be faced with an ordeal as you have never experienced before; My enemies will try to buy you for themselves with insidious speeches, the evil one is at his work already and Destruction is not far away from you; the pope* will have much to suffer...

> ... if anyone comes your way and tells you: "move from your fidelity you have for this pope to another's sound movement," do not move! beware! the yeast of

the Deceiver may be powerful and might taste good, but in reality it is of deadly deception!

... you will be in a spiritual war as never before with an army which originates from the powers of Darkness; pray, My beloved ones, all the time; I Am is with you.... (March 17, 1993; VI, pp. 104f. * Vassula's note: "John Paul II")

Conclusion

In conclusion, I have tried to make three main points. First, that genuine Marian apparitions are works of God given to enliven the Church. In them, God is making us aware of his presence and his grace. To reject them can be to reject grace and to distance oneself in some measure from God - a measure that depends on the role God meant for them to play in our life.

Secondly, the Church has exercised its judgment in the case of some apparitions, and the earnest believer ought to let his own judgment be guided by the Church. When an apparition has been approved by the Church as firmly as have Lourdes and Fatima, to reject it is to dissociate oneself in some measure from the Church itself. It does not mean separation from the Church, but simply that one is declining that *sentire cum Ecclesia* that is the heart of Christian life and Christian wisdom.

Third, that apparitions pertain to the theologian, not so much as subject matter for him to treat, nor as arguments to which he might appeal, but as nourishment for his personal spiritual life, on which his theology is profoundly (if indirectly) dependent.

Appendix

POPE LEO XIII AND DIVINE INSPIRATIONS

Pope Leo XIII

One of the weightiest witnesses to the serious role which extraordinary heaven-sent messages are meant to play in the life of the Church (whether via apparitions or otherwise) is Pope Leo XIII (1878-1903). He had a brilliant gift for dealing skillfully with human problems. It was his successful treatment of a series of difficult situations, first while only a student, then as papal delegate to Benevento and Perugia, as nuncio to Brussels, and finally as bishop of Perugia, that led to his election as Pope. At a time of difficult relationships with the governments of Italy, France, Belgium, Germany, Austria and Russia (to name only the principal ones), he succeeded in winning the respect of international leaders everywhere. In an age when lovers of tradition were often disconcerted by the democratic forms of government taking shape in America and Europe, he led the Church in responding positively to them. His encyclical, *Rerum Novarum*, (1891) is probably more important than any other single factor in bringing the Gospel light to bear on the economic and social problems of the industrial age. At a moment when the western world was being rent by a hardening clash between capital and labor, the encyclical firmly rejected the inevitability of class warfare and defended, on the one hand, the right to private property, and on the other, the right of laborers to a just wage, to humane working conditions and to form trade unions. So insightful and fruitful was this document that subsequent popes issued their own documents to commemorate its 40th,[98] 50th,[99] 70th,[100] 80th,[101] and 100th[102] anniversaries. In this and *Quod Apostolici Muneris* (1878) the dangers of Marxist socialism were firmly pointed out. Other prescient Leonine documents on human liberty, marriage, civil government, the constitution of states, citizenship, slavery, democracy and "the evils affecting modern society," formed the lasting nucleus of what has come to be called the "social teaching" of the Church.[103] In no way could this Pope be accused of a sentimental piety out of touch with the real world.

Yet his papacy was more influenced by what may be called private divine communications than perhaps any other pope since Gregory XI returned to Rome at the prodding of Catherine of Siena. A German nun serving as superior to a convent in Oporto, Portugal, Blessed Maria Droste zu Vischering (Sister Mary of the Divine Heart), wrote to the Pope that Jesus himself had told her he wanted the entire world consecrated to his Sacred Heart. Leo XIII was deeply moved by her request and, after a theological investigation, announced the consecration "of the entire human community to the most Sacred Heart of Jesus" in the encyclical letter, *Annum Sacrum* (1899).[104] The Pope later called this "the most important act" of his pontificate.

Another major act was the fruit of an appeal made by an Italian nun, Sister Elena Guerra, who has since been beatified by Pope John XXIII. Foundress of the Oblate Sisters of the Holy Spirit, she centered her spiritual life on the Holy Spirit, grieving over the fact that he was so little known. Feeling impelled to write about this matter to the Holy Father, she sought counsel and was told that such a project would be out of order. She set the matter aside until eight years later, when a cleaning woman employed by her school declared that it seemed to her that Jesus wanted Elena to write to

---

[98] Pope Pius XI, *Quadragesimo Anno* (May 15, 1931).

[99] Pope Pius XII, radio address of June 1, 1941.

[100] Pope John XXIII, *Mater et Magistra* (1961).

[101] Pope Paul VI, *Octogesima Adveniens* (1971).

[102] Pope John Paul II, *Centesimus Annus* (1991).

[103] See the comments on this point by Pope John Paul II in *Centesimus Annus*, 2 and Passim (Encyclical letter of May 13, 1991).

[104] Cf. Timothy O'Donnell, S.T.D., *Heart of the Redeemer* (Ignatius Press, 1992), p. 158.

the Pope, asking him to promote devotion to the Holy Spirit. There-upon Elena, after consultation with her spiritual director, did write to the Holy Father, urging him to ask the Bishops of the Church to promote the practice of treating the days after the Ascension as a novena of preparation for the feast of Pentecost. Pope Leo responded by a letter officially endorsing her idea of a "new cenacle."[105] He also instructed his counsellors that, if this nun (whom he had never met) had any other such lights that might serve for the good of souls, they should be communicated to him. Emboldened by this response, Sister Elena wrote again, urging that the practice be es-tablished throughout the Church as a "permanent and universal Cenacle." Six months later, the encyclical, *Divinum Illud Munus* (1897) appeared, bemoaning the fact that the Holy Spirit is so little known and appreciated, summarizing more lengthily than any pope had ever done the doctrine of the Church about the Holy Spirit, and prescribing that every parish church should prepare for the feast of Pentecost by a novena of prayer - a practice that was followed until the simplification of the liturgy prescribed by Vatican II.[106]

Finally, a vision that the Pope himself received motivated him to compose a prayer to St. Michael the Archangel and prescribe its use. Father Domenico Pechenino[107] recounts how the Holy Father, while making his thanksgiving after Mass, suddenly straightened up and turned pale, while staring intently at something in the air. Then abruptly he arose and strode into his office, followed by anxious as-sistants who thought he was sick. His private secretary, Msgr. Rinaldo Angeli, recounted the story many times in the presence of the future Cardinal Nasalli Rocca, who wrote about it in his Pastoral Letter for Lent of 1946, in which he says that the Pope apparently had a vision of infernal demons encircling the city of Rome. After half an hour in his office, the Pope emerged with the text of the prayer:

---

[105] Brief of May 5, 1895 (*Acta Sanctae Sedis* XXVII [1894-95], 645-647).

[106] A full account of this matter is given by Léon Cristiani in *Apôtre du Saint-Esprit*, Paris, Apostolat des Editions, 1963. In English, there seems to be little about Elena other than the article, "A woman and the Pope," by Valerian Gaudet, *New Covenant* (Oct. 1973), pp. 4-6.

[107] Father Amorth (cited in the following note) attributes this account to an article by Father Pechenino in *Ephemerides Liturgicae*, 1955. I have not been able to find it there, or in any other issue of that review from 1945 to 1960.

St. Michael, archangel, defend us in battle. Be our protection against the wickedness and snares of the devil. May God rebuke him, we humbly pray; and do thou, O prince of the heavenly host, cast down into hell Satan and all the evil spirits who go about the world seeking the destruction of souls.

The Pope gave instructions that this prayer was to be recited by every priest at the end of each low Mass - a practice that was maintained until the liturgical reforms initiated by Vatican II.[108]

In the official documentation about these acts there is no reference to the supernatural inspirations and experiences that elicited them. This is as it should be; for the foundation for any authoritative acts of the Pope must always reside in Scripture and Church tradition. But that does mean that the inspirations have no real role. On the contrary, they can be crucial in drawing the Holy Father's attention to a point he might otherwise have neglected, in motivating him to choose a given course of action in preference to others, or in other ways. So likewise their role in the Church at large: they always presuppose the revelation and institutions by which the Church is constituted, and they serve to direct our attention where we have been perhaps negligent, to arouse our fervor where we have become tepid or to incline us to a particular path that we may not have taken on our own. Thus they are a means (among others) used by the Holy Spirit in his on-going work of illuminating, consoling and motivating his Church.

---

[108] This story, which has been told in many places, I have taken from Gabriele Amorth, *Un Exorciste Raconte*. Paris, O.E.I.L., 1994, Annexe 1. (The Italian original of this work dates from 1991.)

– IV –
DISCERNMENT OF APPARITIONS

In addition to the Marian apparitions and kindred phenomena discussed in the previous chapters, other extraordinary super-natural phenomena not specifically Marian have been reported in the lives of people such as Conception Cabrera de Amida ("Conchita," 1862-1937), Padre Pio (1887-1968), Teresa Neumann (1898-1962), Yvonne-Aime de Malestroit (1901-1951), Alexandria da Costa (1904-1955), Sister Faustina (1905-1938), Gino Burresi (1932-), and many others. The frequency of such reports seems to be one of the characteristics of our age. But how are we to know in such matters what is real and what is spurious?

Padre Pio

Adopting what they call a 'scientific' approach grounded on sociology and psychology, some critics observe blithely that, in time of stress, people begin concocting fantasies as a way of escape. Such a diagnosis comes from people who haven't looked seriously at the evidence, and assume *a priori* that there is a naturalistic explanation for everything. A believing Christian cannot adopt such a stance since Christianity is rooted in apparitions and prophetic messages as we saw in chapter 3. They are found throughout the New Testament and continued on in the life of the Church thereafter. To be closed to apparitions is to be closed to Christianity itself.

There are also people willing to believe in the older, accepted apparitions, such as Lourdes and Fatima, but who are closed to all that is happening today. Their attitude seems to resemble that of the pharisees and sadducees, who believed in Moses and the prophets, but did not recognize the Messiah standing in person before them.

But one who has an open mind still has need for caution. Jesus warned against false Christs and false prophets working signs and wonders (Mt 24:24). This helps us to understand those Catholics that are very devout and attached to Church traditions, but extremely reluctant to accept anything new, whether it be charisms, visions or even changes in the liturgy officially approved by the Church, such as Eucharistic ministers. I know a number of such persons, whom I profoundly respect. The root of their attitude is good and healthy: a determination to hold faithfully to the religion handed down to us from Jesus. This is far better than to be always looking for something new because the old seems boring. But when faithfulness hardens into rigidity, it deprives us of some very precious graces.

What makes apparitions and locutions particularly difficult to judge is the fact that very often we have to deal with something that is neither completely false or totally authentic, but a mixture of both. While there seem to have been some great imposters in the history of what is called "spiritualism," it is my impression that, where Marian apparitions are concerned, there are not many cases of deliberate and outright fraud. Much more frequent are people deluded through wishful thinking or fanaticism. Conversely, even genuine experiences are often flawed or compromised because of the human imperfections of the subject. Even St. Joan of Arc recanted for a moment, out of fear of the stake.[109] The visions of Anne Catherine Emmerich contain many elements that seem to be legendary rather than historical.[110] Even the books of Sacred Scripture, although guaranteed in their proper message by the Spirit of Truth himself, contain many misconceptions due to the human writer's imperfect knowledge of history and nature.[111] (The idea

---

[109] John Beever, *St. Joan of Arc*, Doubleday, 1974. Pp. 162-168 in the TAN reprint.

[110] Cf. "Anne Catherine Emmerich," in *Surprising Mystics* by Herbert Thurston, S.J. (London, Burns and Oates, 1955).

[111] This accounts for the very carefully worded statement of the Second Vatican Council: "...the books of Scripture firmly, faithfully and without error, teach that truth which God, for the sake of our salvation, wished to see confided to the sacred Scriptures" (Dogmatic Constitution on Divine Revelation, §11). In affirming inerrancy solely of *those truths which God wished to confide* to the Scriptures, this declaration contrasts significantly with previous unqualified statements of the magisterium on the inerrancy of Scripture.

that the sky is set on pillars, Ps. 26:11, or that the earth has "ends," Ps. 47:11, are a couple of the most obvious examples.)

Furthermore, genuine apparitions sometimes stir up false imitations that can compromise them. Thus, after Bernadette saw the lady at the grotto of Lourdes, about forty other people reported that they were having visions too.[112] We can be sure that whatever genuine apparitions are reported today will lead susceptible minds to imagine similar experiences for themselves. But here too we must be cautious about leaping to conclusions. When the apparitions in Beauraing, Belgium, were followed a month or so later by others in the nearby village of Banneux, people naturally suspected that the second series was merely an imitation of the first; but investigation showed that both of them are solidly grounded.[113]

A believing Christian therefore needs to approach such reports with an open mind, but also with caution. But how do you exercise serious discernment when confronted with such an immense number of reports? The Holy See itself is overwhelmed; how can the ordinary Christian succeed?

We can mitigate the difficulty considerably by recognizing that no one needs to pass judgment on all the apparitions. Not even the Church attempts to do this. It is good to study those that seem to have a particular relevance to us - perhaps because they are in some way close to us, perhaps because we know people who have been affected by them, or simply because, for reasons we may not understand, this or that apparition has a special appeal to us. But we don't have to concern ourselves with them all, and so long as we are sincerely open, we need not fear that those we neglect will mean a serious loss to our religious life. The substance of our faith is given in the doctrine of the Church and the sacraments; apparitions do not add to these. They can be helpful in motivating us to a greater appreciation of the Eucharist or Reconciliation, for example; but we are never going to be lacking in anything essential because of some apparition we neglected to investigate.

---

[112] R. Laurentin, Lourdes, *Documents Authentiques*, vol. II, p. 88 (Paris, Lethielleux, 1957).

[113] The apparitions of Beauraing took place from November 29, 1932 to January 3, 1933; those of Banneux from January 15 to March 2, 1933. The Bishop of Namur affirmed the authenticity of the Beauraing apparitions on July 2, 1949. The Bishop of Liège did likewise for Banneux, August 22, 1949. Cf. Omer Englebert, *Dix Apparitions de La Vierge*, Paris, A. Michel 1960, pp. 219, 225.

Secondly, we should remember that the bishop is the chief judge of these matters in his own diocese. As the principal pastor, he has the responsibility, the grace and the means to pass judgment on matters affecting the religious life of his people. By and large, we would do well to rely on his judgment, especially when he has conducted a serious investigation.

Even as I say that, I am acutely conscious of the fact that two successive bishops of Mostar have made vehemently negative judgments about Medjugorje, and I continue to believe in Medjugorje nevertheless. This does not contradict the principle of the bishop's authority; it is an occasion to observe that a bishop is not infallible; he does not have the final word. (When the Bishop of Mostar came out against Medjugorje, the Archbishop of Split spoke up for it,[114] as also numerous other bishops from our own country and elsewhere have done.) Similarly, at Garabandal, four successive bishops were hostile, then the fifth, who was by far better informed than his predecessors, was favorable.[115] This is not said to belittle the authority of bishops, but simply to help delimit their due place, their real but limited authority, in the religious life of the faithful. When all is said and done, it remains that most of us most of the time will do best to rely on the judgment of the appropriate bishop.

But it is also possible to exaggerate reliance on Church authorities. Some people refuse to give any consideration whatsoever to a reported apparition until it has been officially approved. This is not the attitude which the Church asks of us, and it can deprive us of the graces brought by the apparition. The Church normally waits a long time before issuing a pronouncement about a particular apparition, and about most of them it says nothing whatsoever. If we refuse to pay any heed to one until it has been approved, the chances are that we will never have that opportunity. Father John Mary Foster C.S.J. observes that if the shepherds at Bethlehem had waited for the Sanhedrin's approval of the angels' apparition, they would never have seen the baby Jesus.

---

[114] See, for example, "In-depth interview regarding the reported apparitions of our Blessed Mother in Medjugorje..." Dec. 16 to 17, 1984, with Dr. Frane Franic, Archbishop of ... Split, distributed by the Center for Peace, Boston, MA. Cf. ch. 7 of *Medjugorje. Facts, Documents Theology*, by Michael O'Carroll, C.S.Sp. (Veritas, Dublin, 1986).

[115] Christopher Morris, "Why a New Investigation?" *Garabandal* (magazine) Jan.-March 1989, pp. 5-8.

Moreover, this would actually hinder the action of the Church, which looks especially at the fruits when evaluating such phenomena. If everyone waited for the Church to make a pronouncement, there would be no fruits, and in fact no occasion for the Church to make any judgment at all. If people had waited until the Church pronounced on Lourdes or Fatima, we would not have heard of either of them today. Respect for the pastoral authority of the bishop does not mean denying to lay people any judgment whatsoever, but giving to each the due measure of respect.

But to make our own personal judgment about a given apparition is not easy. There are no automatic formulas, no simple litmus tests we can use. Discernment is a work of prudence - not human prudence but the wisdom of the Holy Spirit. There are criteria that help, but they don't give automatic results. Moreover, each case presents different sorts of problems and will be probably be resolved by different tests.

In 1978, the Sacred Congregation for the Doctrine of the Faith, headed by Cardinal Seper, issued a set of guidelines for bishops to use in investigating reports of apparitions and revelations. A report on these guidelines by Father René Laurentin was given at the National Medjugorje Conference at Notre Dame in 1989.[116] While intended for the use of official committees, this document gives indications that can be useful for everyone. There is not space to go into all of them here, so I will select some of the more important instances.

The first admonition given by the Sacred Congregation is to take care to establish the facts. Did the claimed supernatural event actually occur? This obvious, common-sense rule can save much unnecessary excitement. Stories about supernatural phenomena tend to get exaggerated and over-dramatized. Hence, when you are shown photographs of signs in the sky, of faces in a rose blossom or of luminous shapes resembling the Blessed Mother, it is wise to ascertain who took the picture, when and where. Photographs in par-

---

[116] René Laurentin, *The Church and Apparitions - Their Status and Function: Criteria and Reception*, The Riehle Foundation (P.O.B. 7, Milford OH 45150), 1989. A brief commentary on these guidelines by Rev. Frederick Jelly O.P., "Discerning the miraculous norms for judging apparitions and private revelations," was published in *Marian Studies* XLIV (1993) by The Marian Library, University of Dayton, Dayton OH 45469-1390, pp. 41-55.

ticular can easily be altered. When a miraculous healing is reported, make sure the person was really sick, and that the healing lasted. When someone shows you a rosary that has turned to gold, make sure it is not simply the silverplating that has worn off.

One of the most important criteria in judging apparitions is truthfulness. The Congregation cites two kinds of error which would be negative signs: error about the event itself and error in doctrine. No mention is made of what might be called errors in speech. I call attention to this, even though it would seem rather obvious, because some people may be disturbed by the faulty English used in the messages of people such as Vassula or Therese Lopez. Just as the Holy Spirit, in inspiring the biblical authors, used their habitual language (e.g. St. Mark's bad Greek and St. Paul's incoherent style), so likewise Jesus and Mary do not correct the language of their spokesmen. Faulty grammar is not an objection against the authenticity of inspired messages, which is why the Sacred Congregation does not even mention the matter.

Doctrinal errors, however, are much more serious. The revelation given by God through his Son, Jesus Christ, is the standard by which all subsequent revelations are to be measured. Anything that conflicts with the doctrine of Christ can be set aside as certainly not authentic.

In practice, this usually amounts to asking whether the message is in accord with the teaching of the Church. Some may find it presumptuous to propose Church teaching as the standard for passing judgment on a revelation, but this follows directly from what we believe about the Church as a divine mystery. It is not just a community of disciples doing their best to follow the teachings of the master. Amidst all its human shortcomings, the Church is something mysterious and sacred, molded by the hands of Jesus himself, enlightened and sanctified by the Paraclete, the Spirit of Jesus. Individual Christians can err; groups of Christians can err both in doctrine and in behavior; but the Church itself is maintained in the truth by the Holy Spirit. It is, as the First Letter to Timothy declares, "the pillar and foundation of truth" (3:15).

Doctrinal fidelity, however, is not to be identified with theological precision. The "errors" which Father Mitch Pacwa, S.J., for example, points out[117] in the writings of Vassula sometimes appear to be the kind of defective expressions often encountered in someone who lacks theological training, rather than genuine errors in doctrine. More often, they are not even erroneous, but simply an illustration of the inadequacy of human language to express the divine mysteries.

Thus, Father Pacwa cites as heretical the statements Vassula attributes to Jesus, "The Father and I are one and the same," and "the Holy Spirit and I are one and the same." But since Vassula's writings on the whole clearly differentiate between the Father, Son and Holy Spirit, as Father Pacwa himself acknowledges, the texts just cited should not be understood as denying the distinction of the divine persons, but simply as insisting on their unity. The language is not that of scholastic theology, but then neither was the language Jesus used on earth when he said, "The Father and I are One (Jn 10:30)," nor that of St. Paul when he wrote, "the Lord is the Spirit" (II Cor. 3:17).

Similarly, Father Pacwa objects that Jesus' statement, "I have no physical body, I am Spirit," is a denial of the bodily resurrection. But elsewhere Vassula plainly expresses belief in the resurrection; hence it would seem only fair to understand the present statement as an attempt to stress that the glorified body in heaven differs from the body in its present earthly condition. St. Paul contended with the same difficulty when he wrote, "It is sown a natu-

---

[117] "A Critique of a Visionary," by Father Mitch Pacwa, S.J., *Catholic Twin Circle*, August 1, 8, and 15, 1993.

Father Pacwa's view has subsequently been reinforced, but also modified, by the Congregation for the Doctrine of the Faith. In a notification dated October 6, 1995, it cited "several doctrinal errors" in Vassula's writings, the first of which consists in "ambiguous language in speaking of the persons of the Blessed Trinity." No references are given to examples in Vassula's writings, but presumably the Congregation has in mind the same texts as Father Pacwa. However, ambiguous language, which indeed must be acknowledged in certain of these texts when taken in isolation, is hardly to be equated with doctrinal error.

The other errors cited are, in my opinion, either not errors at all, or are not found in Vassula's writing, as I have tried to show in an article, "Vassula and the CDF," which has not yet appeared in print. But should the Church make a solemn judgment that doctrinal error is to be found in Vassula's writings, this woulld indeed disqualify them as authentic revelations.

ral body, it is raised a spiritual body" (I Cor. 15:44). In fact, St. Paul's Greek says literally, "It is sown a physical body," and Vassula, whose native language is Greek rather than English, could very well be understanding the English *physical* in the sense of St. Paul's Greek. In sum, the use of inappropriate language is not to be equated with the doctrinal error which the Sacred Congregation cites as a "negative sign."

Another type of error not dealt with by the Sacred Congregation consists in erroneous predictions. Scripture itself declares that, "even though a prophet speaks in the name of Yahweh, if his oracle is not fulfilled or verified, it is an oracle which Yahweh did not speak" (Deut. 18:22). Many doomsday seers have rightfully been discredited when their predictions were not fulfilled, for example, William Miller in announcing that the Second coming would take place in 1843-44.

Nevertheless, this criterion is not as simple and facile as might appear. Jonah was sent to announce that Nineveh would be destroyed in forty days; but because the people of Nineveh fasted, God "repented of the evil that he had threatened to do to them; he did not carry it out" (Jonah 3:10), as Jonah himself had foreseen. St. Thomas Aquinas explains that sometimes what God reveals to the prophet is not the event that is actually going to take place, but the causes which of themselves would lead to it, while the possibility remains open that something could still intervene to prevent it.[118]

Also, there can be slight chronological disparities which at first seem to belie the message, but in retrospect are of little import. At Garabandal, Conchita announced that the "miracle of the host" would take place on July 18. When it had not occurred by the end of the day, some people left disillusioned. But it occurred in fact an hour and three quarters after midnight, having been delayed because of an indecent dance going on in the village. Similarly, at Fatima, in foretelling the great miracle of October 13, Mary told the children she would appear at noon, whereas she actually came about 1:30 P.M.[119] Likewise at Fatima Mary told Lucia that the Second World War would begin in the reign of Pius XI. This Pope

---

[118] *Summa Theologiae*, II-II, Q. 171, art. 6, reply to the second objection.

[119] Joseph Pelletier, *Our Lady Comes to Garabandal*, Assumption Publications, Worcester MA 1971, p. 106.

died on February 13, 1939, whereas war was not officially declared until November 3, when Pius XII had succeeded to the papacy. But serious arguments have been made that the war really began when Hitler marched into Austria in March of 1938, or even when he occupied the Rhineland in March of 1936.[120]

Likewise prophets can be simply defective, and even while rightly announcing a future event shown them by God, introduce minor errors of their own, particularly in regard to dates, which God seldom reveals. Thus errors about dates, particularly when viewed from a short range, although certainly posing problems, may not always constitute decisive disqualifications.

The fact that a message is doctrinally sound is, of course, no guarantee that it is supernatural; it may mean only that the visionary knows his catechism. However, when messages are long or numerous, touching on many different subjects, especially when the visionary has had little education, it becomes less and less likely that an illusion can be sustained without error. How many ordinary Catholics would be able to fabricate spiritual messages like those of Medjugorje, day after day, then week after week, and finally month after month, for fourteen years, without slipping into error? (And we must bear in mind that the visionaries were all teenagers, one of them only 11, at the beginning of the apparitions, and living under a communist regime that made it impossible for them to receive a thorough Catholic education.)

Mary of Agreda composing The City of God

Even in regard to doctrinal fidelity, the Congregation points out that we must take into consideration the point made by St. Ignatius in his *Spiritual Exercises* (n. 336), that "the subject may

---

[120] Frère Michel de la Sainte Trinité, *The Whole Truth about Fatima*, vol. II, p. 696 (Immaculate Heart Publications, Box 1028, Buffalo NY 14205).

unconsciously add human elements to authentic supernatural revelation." Thus the accounts of the Blessed Virgin's life composed by St. Brigid of Sweden, Venerable Mary of Agreda and Anne Catherine Emmerick, contradict one another on various points;[121] nonetheless, they are widely regarded as authentic revelations.

Besides the objective truthfulness of the messages, the Sacred Congregation also calls attention to the subjective qualities of the seer as helpful criteria. One is whether the visionary is "able to return to the normal regime of faith." This amounts to asking whether he or she is able to live without visions. If someone needs extraordinary experiences in order to stay on a spiritual high, this is a very bad sign. Like every other Christian, the visionary has to make his way into heaven by a life of faith, humility and charity. At Medjugorje, the visionaries insist that the Blessed Mother told them to place a much higher value on receiving Jesus in the Eucharist than on seeing her.[122] That should be the attitude of every visionary. In fact, those that are genuine often regret very much that they have been chosen for a mission that takes them out of the ordinary way of Christian life.

Another criterion listed by the Sacred Congregation is whether the visionary is mentally balanced. "Psychic illness or psychopathic tendencies that have surely exercised an influence" on the phenomenon in question would be a negative sign. Common sense cautions us to be slow to believe someone who seems to have mental or emotional disorders.

However, even on this point, the Congregation is very cautious, leaving room for the possibility of a genuine apparition to a person with psychological problems. That would seem to be the reason for specifying that the pathology is a negative sign only when it has *certainly* influenced the phenomenon under question. In fact, I personally have known an emotionally disturbed person who gave very strong indications of having received genuine messages from Our Lady. This would be altogether in accord with Our

---

[121] Raphael Brown, in the introduction to *The Life of Mary as Seen by the Mystics* (TAN, Rockford, 1991), without being a very critical study of the matter, cites covenient testimonies of numerous serious scholars on this point.

[122] Note also Vicka's statement, "the Blessed Mother has led me to understand that the center of my life is the Eucharist," in *Queen of the Cosmos* by Jan Connell (Paraclete Press, Orleans MA, 1990) p. 69.

Lord's own stated policy of bending down to those who are weakest and lowliest.

The Congregation goes on to ask whether the visionary is honest, upright and sincere. If he is self-seeking, trying to draw attention to himself or to impose his own way on others, these would be negative indications. (During the Pope's visit to Denver, a man asked me to help him get permission to speak to the Holy Father because, he said, "I am a visionary." Although he had newspaper articles about himself to prove his claim, I was not greatly impressed.) On the other hand, it would be going too far to say that an authentic visionary must be a saint. God may very well choose to reveal himself through imperfect instruments, and those who have met the contemporary visionaries often confirm that this is indeed the case with them - something the visionaries themselves readily admit.

Sister Faustina

A criterion that requires more extended discussion is the visionary's obedience to Church authority - a different matter from fidelity to Catholic doctrine. Some may be disturbed by this requirement, asking, "Are there not times when the Church itself is wayward and needs to be called back to the true path by prophets and visionaries stirred up by the Holy Spirit?" And won't these inevitably be in conflict with actual Church teaching and practice? Aren't they almost sure to be condemned by those very authorities they were inspired to rebuke? To back up such a concern, there are examples such as St. Joan of Arc, condemned to death by an ecclesiastical court presided over by the Bishop of Beauvais; or the message of Divine Mercy, as proposed by Sister Faustina, suppressed by the Holy Office itself.[123]

---

[123] *Acta Apostolicae Sedis* 51 (1959), p. 271.

In the seven Letters to the Churches in the Book of the Apocalypse, Jesus speaking through St. John declares to the Church of Ephesus: "You have lost the love you had at first. Realize how far you have fallen. Repent, and do the works you did at first" (Apoc. 2:4-5). Mary seems to be echoing this message today, as her apparitions seek to shake us out of our lethargy, rekindle our fervor, and reprimand our faults. Sometimes it is those who hold authority in the Church that are particularly in need of reform; and we have already noted that clergy tend to be particularly skeptical about the reports of supernatural phenomena.[124] If the visionaries are required to submit to Church authority, isn't it likely that God's message will be suppressed by the very ones who need to hear it? When the Sanhedrin ordered the apostles to stop preaching about the Resurrection, St. Peter retorted, "We must obey God rather than men" (Acts 5:29). One may wonder whether modern visionaries, when ordered to be silent, may not be entitled, or even obligated, to make the same response.

This complex, delicate problem needs to be dealt with one step at a time. The first and most basic is to recognize that Christ himself put pastors in charge of his flock. (*Pastors* refers primarily to bishops, who are the principal pastors of their dioceses. In a lesser measure the heads of parishes also have this role.) Jesus wants his flock to be led by the pastors he has put over them (Acts 20:28) and it is essential to the health of the Church that this be so. No doubt, the Holy Spirit works directly in the hearts of the faithful and not only through pastors; hence certain types of Pentecostal Christians decline to obey any human authority, claiming to be led directly by the Holy Spirit. But this is a false dichotomy. The same Jesus who sends the Holy Spirit is the Jesus who appointed shepherds to act in his name. Catholic tradition insists that one of the surest indications that a person is led by the Holy Spirit is that he be obedient to his pastor. Such a one is being pastored by Jesus himself.

Throughout the history of the Church genuinely prophetic spirits have always been humble and faithful in obedience to their due superiors. Some famous examples are Teresa of Avila, Catherine of Siena and John of the Cross; more recent ones are Padre Pio and Sister Faustina. Jesus himself assured the latter that she did right in

---

[124] Cf. chapter 3.

Teresa of Avila

obeying her superiors when they forbade her to carry out what he had told her to do.[125] At Medjugorje, each time the Bishop of Mostar forbade that apparitions be received in a particular place - first the sacristy then the presbytery - the visionaries obeyed him.[126] In a similar situation at Garabandal, Mary herself respected the bishop's directive leading the little visionaries in ecstasy around the outside of the church, but never taking them in.[127] By contrast, when the "seer" of Necedah, Mary Ann Van Hoof, together with her associates, was placed under interdict by Bishop Freking, she brought in a schismatic bishop to create a new diocese for her. (Yet even he, as well as his successor, eventually denounced her.)[128]

Secondly, we should bear in mind that the obedience called for is the *virtue* of obedience. This does not require that you submit to anyone whatsoever in everything he tells you to do; it means obeying legitimate authority in matters to which this authority extends. If a pastor goes beyond his limits, there is no obligation to obey him.

Sometimes it is difficult to know exactly where one is bound to obey and where not. Hence the anguish of Joan of Arc, Catherine Labouré, or Sister Faustina, who were at times uncertain what their obligations were when human superiors opposed the orders received from Jesus. It would be impossible here to define the limits of pastoral authority, which involve many complex technical questions.

---

[125] *Divine Mercy in My Soul. The Diary of Sister M. Faustina Kowalska* (Marian Press, Stockbridge MA, 1987) #645 and *passim*.

[126] Cf. R. Laurentin, *7 Années d'Apparitions* (Paris, O.E.I.L. 1988) p. 20.

[127] Cf. "Obedience to the Church," ch. 12 of *God Speaks at Garabandal* by Joseph Pelletier, A.A. (Assumption Publication, Worcester MA, 1971).

[128] Patrick Slattery, "The Apparitions that Never Were," *Today's Catholic*, Sept. 1, 1991, p. 10.

But it is also unnecessary; what matters chiefly is that the person in question make a sincere effort to obey in those matters wherein he is obligated. The anguish of being uncertain where duty lies cannot always be avoided; as a way of our sharing in the cross of Christ, it will be coredemptive if we bear it with faith.

What if a pastor who is closed to supernatural phenomena tries to suppress an authentic apparition? If the visionary obeys him, wouldn't that interfere with the divine plan? To resolve this problem, we need to recall that Christian obedience is based on faith in God who has many ways to ensure that his plans be accomplished in spite of obstacles of whatever sort. Sometimes by an interior light he moves the pastor to change his mind and grant the permission which at first had been refused. Thus the Bishop of Mexico at first did not believe in Juan Diego, but later on he did.[129] At other times, God has been known to remove the pastor from office so as to clear the way. Or he may simply act by another route. When the Pope refused to accept St. Bridget of Sweden's word that God wanted him to return to Rome, Catherine of Siena was sent, with greater success. When the authorities in Paris did not give much heed to the revelations made to St. Catherine Labouré, Mary began working in Lourdes the miracles she would have done in Paris had the authorities been more cooperative.[130]

I can't help but wonder if there is not a similar relationship between Garabandal and Medjugorje. Both foretell a warning, a sign and a chastisement. It would seem plausible that, because the message of Garabandal went almost unheeded when it came out in 1964, Mary repeated it more dramatically at Medjugorje in 1981.

In any event, we never need to fear that we will hinder God's plan by obeying our lawful superiors, even if they seem closed to the supernatural. Rather, we can be sure that our obedience itself, and the sacrifice it entails, will contribute to God's work.

There are other criteria listed by the Sacred Congregation which do not require any discussion here. On the positive side: "Healthy

---

[129] Cf. *The Wonder of Guadalupe* by Francis Johnston (TAN, Rockford IL, 1981) ch. 2.

[130] When news of the events at Lourdes reached Catherine Labouré's convent, Catherine remarked, "If the superiors had been willing, the Blessed Virgin would have chosen our chapel." (R. Laurentin, *Vie de Catherine Labouré*, Desclée de Brouwer, Paris, 1980, p. 148).

devotion and rich, lasting spiritual fruits (e.g. the spirit of prayer, conversions, works of charity, etc.)" On the negative side: "evident seeking of financial advantage closely connected with the event," and "gravely immoral acts committed at the time or on the occasion of the event by the subject (i.e. the supposed visionary) or his followers."[131]

The criteria given by the Sacred Congregation have a kind of universality. They can be applied to any apparition whatsoever (although some will be more relevant in one case and others in another). They are in a sense basic principles for discernment. But besides such general criteria, there are often little signs which, without necessarily being decisive, may be very revealing about a particular apparition, but unlikely to occur in others. This is especially the case with negative signs.

Thus at Necedah, Wisconsin, the Blessed Virgin, in condemning the evil of abortion, is reported to have exclaimed to the seer, Mary Ann Van Hoff, "What will happen to the future white generations if the white people do not stand up and be willing to bear their own children."[132] The implicit racism of such a remark is hardly what one would expect from the Mother of God. At Bayside, New York, one of "Mary's messages" to Veronica Leuken declared that Pope Paul VI was a prisoner in the Vatican, his mind dulled by medication, while his place was being taken by an imposter who has been fashioned into Paul Pope's likeness by plastic surgery. This was all the work of three "agents of Satan," cardinals Casaroli, Villot and Benelli. As a consequence, the faithful were not bound to obey the directives issued at Rome under the name of the Pope.[133] While one cannot say that such a development is intrinsically impossible, its implausibility could make a person hesitate somewhat over the apparitions.

Likewise, at both Necedah and Bayside, the charismatic renewal was pronounced to be the work of Satan. For those who are

---

[131] A spurious example of the latter is dealt with by Fr. Laurentin on p. 11 of his 1989 publication.

[132] *The Apparitions of the Blessed Virgin Mary at Necedah, Wisconsin, U.S.A.* (a pamphlet published and distributed by the Necedah shrine), November 1982, p. 8.

[133] "Apparitions at Bayside. Sept. 27, 1975," in the quarterly *Michael* (Rougemont, Que., Canada), Oct.-Dec. 1975, pp. 5 & 6.

well acquainted with the charismatic renewal, this might be sufficient to discredit the apparitions (but obviously, this criterion would not bear weight for everyone).

At the White Cross apparition site in Spain, the seer, Rosario Arenillas, is reported to have exclaimed in the course of one of his visions, "Father, Father!... Come down a little more, as I can scarcely hear Your Voice." Later on he added, "Your hands are cold, my Father."[134] Such `experiences' seem highly implausible in association with a God who can speak directly to human hearts, and who does not ordinarily use hands.

In Australia, there is a "seer" who uses the name, "The Little Pebble," to conceal his identity. The employment of such a name, especially when it is overtly "humble" or sentimental, is often a sign of pious day-dreaming. The same person transmits the message that "if any Seer throughout the world does not unite with the Apparition here, in Australia, they will fall; no matter how great the Seer may be..."[135] Besides the improbability that Our Lady would refer to the "greatness" of a visionary, the insistence that all other seers acknowledge this one is more redolent of delusions of grandeur than of the humility and modesty characteristic of both the Blessed Virgin and her clients.

The same Little Pebble drew up a "food list for the survival of God's people during the time of the great tribulation, especially after May 1988, which was to be the beginning of it."[136] The topic of dates has already been discussed; here I would point out that, while Mary often speaks of the imminence of the tribulation and chastisement through well-accredited spokesmen, as we have seen in chapter 2, her way of preparing for it consists of prayer, penance and recourse to her Immaculate Heart. The plan of storing up food has the earmarks of a more earthly inspiration.

The prophet Elijah seems to exercise a particular fascination over many dreamers, due no doubt to the fact that he was predicted

---

[134] Narrated in the newsletter, *Our Lady Comes to Australia*, published by "The Little Pebble," POB 1931, Wolongong, N.S.W. 2500, Australia.

[135] *Our Lady Comes to Australia*, no. 88, p. 3 (message of June 1, 1986).

[136] This is in a sheet distributed by a center called, "Our Lady, Queen of all Titles," at P.O.B. 2302, East Chicago, IN, 46312. I have only a clipping without label or date, but it seems to come from the newsletter, *Our Lady Comes to Australia*, cited above.

to return "before the great and dreadful day of the Lord" (Malachi 4:5), a prophecy that Jesus said was fulfilled in the person of John the Baptist (Mat. 17:12). I personally have met three men who claimed either to have a special association with Elijah, or actually to be the prophet himself come back to earth.[137] While it is not possible to speak absolutely about the matter, such pretensions smack more of delusions of grandeur than of serious religious experience.

Similarly, delusionary prophets are often inclined to seek out great and famous people to communicate a message to them. The Holy See receives an unending stream of such messages intended for the Pope.[138] It certainly is possible that some of these might be authentic; we saw in the appendix to chapter 3 that Pope Leo XIII took two such messages quite seriously. Nevertheless, genuine prophets tend to shrink from such exalted missions, and those who seek them out are more likely deluded.

Arrogance likewise is an unfavorable sign. True prophets tend to be humble and respectful, especially when addressing high authorities in the Church or even in the state. St. Catherine of Siena never lost her deep reverence for the Holy Father as "the sweet Christ on earth," even when she had to chide him. But I have seen a letter addressed to the Pope by one who claimed to be a prophet, and who used a tone like that of a school teacher reprimanding a wayward child.

Finally, I would like to call attention to another factor not mentioned by the Sacred Congregation, perhaps because it is not an objective criterion. It is nevertheless of great importance, I believe, especially when we are seeking to make a private, personal appraisal. It may be called the *inner witness of the Spirit*. When a message is from the Lord, it has a way of touching us in such a way that we recognize his voice in it. This was the case with St. Peter, which is why Jesus said to him, "Flesh and blood have not revealed this to you, but my Father who is in heaven" (Mt 16:16). It is undeniable that this witness occurs, and I believe that it is probably the principal factor leading us to give credence to something

---

[137] I have been fascinated with the thought of bringing these three together for a party, to observe the results!

[138] It was Bishop Paolo Hniliça who told me this when someone asked him to convey such a message.

as coming from God. But it can't be used as an objective argument, and normally needs to be supported by other criteria.

However, it does not follow that a genuine apparition will be recognized by everyone who examines it in good faith. Here too there is room for innocent errors. It may be also that a given apparition is intended for the benefit of a limited group only, not for everyone. Hence, for some people to be attracted by one apparition and others by another is perfectly normal; the Holy Spirit gives different graces to different people. But it is very important that these different attractions not turn into hostile sects or cliques. We should pay heed to those which we believe are from God, while remaining tolerant of those to which others are drawn, at least so long as they have not proved to be evil or harmful. When the devotees of different apparitions become hostile or closed to each other, Satan is the winner and the Church the loser.

Finally, while all the above factors, as well as others not discussed here, are useful for judging apparitions, we must recall again that discernment remains always a prudential judgment. Much learning is no guarantee of good sense. It is chastening to recall that the first major treatise on discernment, one that is still considered a classic, was composed by the brilliant French theologian, Jean Gerson, who, however, misjudged St. Brigid of Sweden and St. Catherine of Siena, two of the greatest visionaries of all time.[139] Similarly, Eusebius Amort, an outstanding German theologian of the 18th century, who wrote the next great treatise on discernment, seems to have erred in regard to Mary of Agreda.[140]

Much more could be said about discernment, but a complete treatise cannot be undertaken here.

---

[139] See chapter 3.

[140] Eusebius Amort, *De Revelationibus et Apparitionibus Privatis*, Augsburg, 1744.

– V –
THE FIFTH LATERAN COUNCIL ON REVELATIONS AND PROPHECIES

I n 1978, the Congregation for the Doctrine of the Faith, headed by Cardinal Seper, sent all the bishops of the Church a four-page document entitled, "Norms ... on how to proceed in judging presumed apparitions and revelations."[141] These norms consti-tute the latest refinement of a stance which the Church began to take at the Fifth Lateran Council in 1516.[142] A review of the position taken by Lateran V and of the occasion which provoked it sheds an interesting light on today's situation and the current legislation.

Lateran V

The Lateran Council denounced preachers who, without serious foun-dation, were warning people about "terrors, threats and many evils" which they claim are "close at hand,"

The Fifth Lateran Council

---

[141] This document, dated February 25, and communicated secretly to the bishops, has never been published officially. Its contents and background were pre-sented by Father René Laurentin at the 1989 National Conference on Medjugorje at the University of Notre Dame, and later published as *The Church and Apparitions* (Milford, Ohio; Riehle Foundation, 1989).
Most of the norms cited in this document are discussed above, in chapter 4.
[142] Concilium Lateranense V, Sessio XI [*Circa Modum Praedicandi*] (19 dec. 1516) in *Conciliorum Oecumenicorum Decreta* (Herder, 1962) pp. 610-614). For an English translation, see *Decrees of the Ecumenical Councils*, ed. by Norman P. Tanner, S.J. (Sheed and Ward and Georgetown U.P. 1990), Vol. 1, pp. 593 ff. However, I have made my own translation of the texts cited.

in fact actually "breaking in upon us." Some claimed that their ideas came "from the prompting or inspiration of the Holy Spirit"; some were trying, "with much shouting... to persuade the people about fabricated miracles, false new prophecies and other trivia hardly different from old wives' tales."

In response to such 'prophetic preaching,' the Council forbade any preacher to speak about "the predetermined time of future evils, or the coming of the antichrist, or a definite day of judgment," adding that "those who have dared to say such things in the past have lied." It was likewise forbidden for anyone "in public sermons to preach other future events from Sacred Scripture, or to affirm that they have these from the Holy Spirit or from divine revelation."

However, the Council kept open the possibility that God might, "by some kind of inspiration, ... reveal ... things that are to happen in the Church of God in the future." But "as an ordinary rule, such claimed inspirations, before being made public or preached to the people, should be understood as reserved from now on to the examination of the Apostolic See." If there is not time for that, the bishop of the place should examine the matter with the aid of three or four learned men.

This is a kind of first sketch of the Church's policy on dealing with private revelations and kindred phenomena. It would seem to be at the root of canon 1399 of the 1917 Code of Canon Law, which declared that "books and pamphlets recounting new apparitions, revelations, visions, prophecies, or miracles" are not to be published without ecclesiastical approval (cf. can. 1395, 1, #2). This requirement was suppressed by Pope Paul VI on October 14, 1970, and replaced by the new instructions issued by the Congregation for the Doctrine of the Faith in 1978, partially discussed in the preceding chapter.

Background of Lateran V

What provoked the Lateran Council to concern itself with preachers who upset people with new prophecies? According to Marjorie Reeves:

> ... in the first quarter of the sixteenth century there was
> a considerable circle of people, centered perhaps mainly

in Rome, who were deeply concerned with the final program of history and looked for World Emperor and Angelic Pope as well as Antichrist.[143]

We will see more about the identity of these figures below. Concern about them did not arise from any single event, but had been welling up all through the fifteenth century:

In ... Italy, general anxiety was building up to a peak in the 1480s and 1490s. Luca Landucci reported a miracle in his Florentine Diary because everyone was awaiting great signs from God. There were wandering prophets crying 'Woe!' in Siena in 1472, and in 1492 Fra Giuliano was inveighing against *l'avara Babilonia* in Milan. Various prophets appeared with strange foreboding messages in the streets of Rome. In 1484 one who posed as a humanist, an astrologer, and a cabbalist rode through proclaiming imminent change to the whole world.[144]

---

[143] Marjorie Reeves, *Prophecy in the Later Middle Ages. A Study of Joachimism* (Oxford, Clarendon, 1969), p. 441. This work is the chief source of the present article, which is largely an attempt to strain out of her immense erudition the information relevant to our topic, and make it accessible to those who haven't time to go through her whole book. I have not been able to check her sources, many of which are to be found in manuscripts or rare books difficult of access. However, Reeves' credentials as a scholar and an authority on Joachimism are unsurpassed. On the other hand, her focus on Joachim gives a certain bias to her work; moreover, she does not seem to take seriously the possibility of genuine prophetic inspiration and the consequent necessity of discerning between authentic and inauthentic prophecies.

Bernard McGinn in *Visions of the End. Apocalyptic Traditions in the Middle Age* (Columbia University Press 1979) supplies a rich collection of texts illustrating this same theme, accompanied by careful presentations of their background.

[144] Reeves, p. 430. Reeves' observation is confirmed by William A. Christian Jr. in a paper read at the Conference on Religion and Religious Movements in the Mediterranean Area (Amsterdam, Dec. 18-20, 1979). After reviewing the apparitions reported in southern Europe during the period following World War II, he remarks that "remarkably similar visions were occurring throughout Southwest Europe... in the period from 1450 to 1515." (My citation is from an unpublished manuscript of the paper, "Religious Apparitions and the Cold War in Southern Europe.")

In 1490 Stefano Infessura announced the coming of "one of unknown nationality, in the poor garb of a mendicant friar, who "this very year" would threaten the Romans with a great calamity which would spread to the rest of Italy. "Three years from now, in the year 1493, there will appear a cleric who has no temporal domain. Then there will be the Angelic Pastor who will care for nothing but the life of souls and spiritual matters."[145]

At this time the Sienese chronicler Tizio wrote a book on the end of the world, whilst, on the other hand, the Florentine canon Prospero Pitti prophesied the renewal of the Church and the advent of the Angelic Pope. In these same years the strange and solemn prophecy attributed to St. Cathaldus was striking like a knell on men's ears, and Paul of Middelburg's astrological prognostications were sweeping through Italy. Again the emphasis here was on catastrophe and Antichrist, yet the conjunction of the stars in 1484 also pointed to the advent of a holy Reformer. A few years later Lichtenberger's *Prognosticatio*, with its popular mixture of astrology and prophecy, was attaining great popularity among Italians, especially in northern Italy."[146]

In 1509 Charles de Bovelles in Spain wrote about the imminent appearance of a reforming pope. In 1512, the year the Council opened, Fray Melchior of Burgos foretold that within five years, the Roman Empire, many kingdoms and the papacy itself would be overturned. All the clergy would be slain except the elect. The Church would be transferred to Jerusalem, after which humanity would live in virtue and happiness.[147]

---

[145] Stefano Infessura, *Diario della Città di Roma*, ed. O. Tommasini (Rome, 1890), pp. 264-5. (Reeves ibid.)

[146] Reeves, ibid.

[147] Reeves, p. 446. An admiring account of this prophecy was sent by Cazala to Cardinal Ximenes de Cisneros, who took an active part in procuring publication of the Bull convening the Fifth Lateran Council. (Cf. "Ximénes de Cisneros," *Catholic Encyclopedia* X, 1912, p. 731a.)

Savonarola

Savonarola

The tone of this period is epitomized perhaps in Savonarola, the fiery Dominican preacher, who, just two decades prior to the Council, was denouncing corruption in the city of Florence. He likewise condemned the immorality of the clergy, including the Roman Curia and Pope Alexander VI. Taking his inspiration in large part from the Apocalypse, he foretold, as summarized by a modern historian, that "the Church would soon be terribly chastized and then renewed.... He had formed the conviction ... that he was a prophet inspired to announce God's judgment on Italy and the Church." The Pope summoned Savonarola to Rome, "to explain the revelations he claimed to have received from God." The friar refused to obey, but offered to send the Pope his recently completed *Compendium Revelationum*. The Pope condemned his claim to divine inspiration, to which Savonarola replied that he had never claimed to be an inspired prophet.[148] Despite Savonarola's excommunication in 1497 and execution the following year, in 1508 there were still preachers in Florence crying, "*grande tribolazione et la novacione della chiesa.*"[149]

The Reform Movement

Behind this multiplication of apocalyptic prophecies lay a widespread distress over the lamentable state of Christendom. Clamor for the reform of Church and society had been building up pressure for several hundred years. Lateran V itself was largely occupied with the *reformatio Ecclesiae*. The very year in which it ended, 1517, Martin Luther's theses, tacked onto the door of the castle

---

[148] K. Foster, "Savonarola," *New Catholic Encyclopedia XII (1967).*
[149] Reeves, p. 438.

church in Wittenberg, ignited the explosion that rendered much of the Council's work irrevelant.

Reform and Prophecy

How yearning for reform fostered apocalyptic prophecies is a speculative question. I can only hazard the suggestion that those whose concern about the evils afflicting Church and society was motivated by religious faith tended naturally to look to God for enlightenment and relief. In Scripture, and especially in its apocalyptic elements, many found an interpretation of what was going on and a promise of what was to come. Some believed that they had been given an answer directly from God. At any rate, it is an historical fact that out of their distress there arose prophecies affirming that the longed for reform would indeed be brought about by the hand of God. Some prophecies depicted the concrete ways, and even the very time frame, in which this purification would take place. In an age in which Church and state were largely intermingled, it is not surprising that the prophecies dealt with secular and ecclesiastical affairs together.

The prophecies revolved largely around the three notions cited in the passage quoted above: the Last World Emperor, the Angelic Pastor, and the Antichrist. Interpretations of these figures varied from one prophecy to another, but it is possible to point out some of the predominant traits.

The Last Great Emperor

The last great emperor was one whose reign would bring forth a flourishing Christianity, with the enemies of the Church either converted or eliminated. Then the emperor would go to Jerusalem and surrender his office to God. Subsequently the Antichrist would appear and reign until his final defeat by the archangel Michael, after which Christ would return in glory.

The earliest evidence we have of such a notion comes in some seventh-century Syrian *Revelations* circulated under the pseudonym of Methodius. Another form of the notion appeared in the tenth century, in the Latin version of the ancient "Tiburtine oracle."[150]

---

[150] A summary of the complex problem of dating this notion can be found in the work of McGinn (cited in note 3 above), pp. 43 ff.

German and French traditions perpetuated diverse notions of the Last Great Emperor. The former expected him to be a German; after the reign of Frederick II (1212-1250), he was often concretized as an expected Frederick III. The French tradition, on the other hand, looked rather for a Second Charlemagne.[151]

The Antichrist

The Antichrist, who was to follow the Last Great Emperor, had a great variety of interpretations. For some authors there would be both a hidden, "mystical" Antichrist who would be a heretic, as well as an open Antichrist, sometimes visualized as a Saracen. When Pope John XXII (1316-1334) condemned the spiritual Franciscans, they retorted by denouncing him as the *Antichristus mysticus*.[152] A number of popular plays about the Antichrist were performed during the fourteenth and fifteenth centuries.[153]

The Angelic Pope

The Angelic Pope was to be a saintly Pontiff who would come one day to reform the Church and introduce an era of general holiness. This expectation seems to have been precipitated largely by the example of Pope Celestine V. This devout monk, elected Pope as a compromise among disputing factions of cardinals, proved to be so incapable of governing the Church that he had to resign in the same year he was elected (1294). Nevertheless his career engendered hope in a saintly Vicar of Christ who would one day restore the Church to holiness. The concept of an Angelic Pope gained in importance during the fourteenth and fifteenth centuries, as the Avignon papacy (1309-1377), the Great Schism (1328-1417) and the general condition of the Church exacerbated the clamor for reform. Some radical groups expected the actual Pope and cardinals to be slain in

---

[151] Reeves 299 ff., 324.

[152] Reeves p. 205. McGinn 207 ff.

[153] These have been studied in the doctoral dissertation, *Antichrist and the Prophets of Antichrist in the Chester Cycle* by Brother Linus Urban Lucken (Catholic University of America, 1940). Cf. Vincent Miceli, S.J., *The Antichrist* (Roman Catholic Books, P.O.B. 255, Harrison, N.Y.).

[154] Reeves p. 414.

preparation for the coming of the Angelic Pope.[154] The Angelic Pope lingered a long time in people's dreams. An *opusculum, De Angelico Pastore*,[155] was composed by the Franciscan Petrus Galatinus some time after the Fifth Lateran Council.

The expectation of an Angelic Pope was sometimes expanded into a series of prophecies about a whole line of future popes. The *Vaticinia de summis pontificibus* purported to be ancient. Critical analysis, however, seems to indicate that they were composed about the time of the death of Pope Benedict XI (1304), because popes previous to that date are depicted in ways readily identifiable, whereas the predictions about subsequent popes (the last six of them 'Angelic') are "imaginary."[156]

A century later (about 1356) another series of papal prophecies was composed by some Fraticelli of Tuscany, who represented the last Pope as the Antichrist.[157] By the sixteenth century, the two lists were combined, and after that revised and republished numerous times,[158] as well as being imitated by many others, of which the 'Prophecy of St. Malachy' is today the best-known example.[159]

Sources

The sources of these predictions are many, and they call for very diverse appraisals. Prominent among them are St. Bridget of Sweden and St. Vincent Ferrer, whose prophetic gifts deserve to be taken very seriously, although their authentic ideas were often distorted in the popularized form in which they were circulated. There was, dominating all the others, Joachim of Fiore, whose prophetic gifts are very suspect. Finally, there was a considerable number of obscure figures who today have scarcely any credentials at all, positive or negative. All of them came to be mixed together in one brew.

---

[155] Petrus Galatinus, *De Angelico Pastore*, MS. Vat., Lat. 5578. The date of this work is not settled. Reeves (p. 44 n. 2) indicates that it is one of the author's latest writings. She calls for a revision of the dating given in *Antonianum*, I, 327-28, by Kleinhans.

[156] Reeves, pp. 193-4, 402-403. A partial translation is given by McGinn, p. 194 ff.

[157] Reeves pp. 214-215; 412-415. Several of the prophecies are given in translation by McGinn, p. 234 ff.

[158] Reeves 415 ff. See also p. 96.

[159] Reeves p. 461. The Prophecy of St. Malachy was first published in *Lignum Vitae* in 1595.

St. Bridget

St. Bridget of Sweden (1303-1373), probably the greatest visionary in the history of the Church, filled seven volumes with the
records of her revelations. Many of them had to do with mysteries
in the life of Jesus and Mary.[160] Most of them related to concrete

situations in her life or that of people
to whom she was sent. Some involved
insight into the state of soul of these
people. To her spiritualized sensibil-
ity, sinners stunk so badly that there
were people before whom she could
not refrain from holding her nose. She
also received admonitions about the
state of society and Church. Jesus told
her that priests, knights and peasants
had been chosen for diverse functions
needed for the good order of society.
If each did his part, all would be well

St. Bridget on pilgrimage

in Christendom. Instead, however, the priests are like lepers, the
knights a terror instead of a protection to society, and the peasants
like asses.[161] Through Bridget, Christ admonished kings and popes
as well as her own relatives and acquaintances. He makes a shock-
ingly harsh appraisal of Pope Clement VI (1342-1352). "You are
worse than the devil," Bridget says to him; and she has a vision of
the Pontiff putrefied and monstrously disfigured.[162] She was likewise frank and severe with kings and queens. But Bridget was not
much inclined to foretelling the future. When a monk set about
proving to her "out of his books" that the time of Antichrist was
very close, Bridget was reassured by the apostle John himself that,
"We know neither the day nor the hour."[163] However, like some of

---

[160] During Bridget's lifetime, her revelations were collected in seven books, the
Liber Coelestis Revelationum. After her death, the *Liber Magnus* was ex-
tracted from these, and about 1433 the brief *Onus Mundi* was compiled by J.
Tortsch of Leipzig. Cf. Johannes Jorgensen, *St. Bridget of Sweden* (London
etc., Longmans, Green, 1954), vol. 1, p. 300 ff.

[161] Jorgensen, vol. I, p. 158.

[162] Ibid. Vol. I, p. 252; vol. II, p. 76.

[163] Ibid. vol. II, p. 114. A similar text is given by McGinn, p. 245f.

our modern visionaries, she expected a terrible chastisement of the Church, to be followed probably by a great Age of the Spirit.[164] In the course of the fifteenth century, Bridget's prophecies became widely disseminated, but also altered and distorted.[165] The solemn approval by the Church of Bridget's supernatural gifts was cited above in chapter 3.[166]

St. Vincent Ferrer

St. Vincent Ferrer O.P. (1350-1419) had a vision of Christ commissioning him to preach penance and prepare mankind for judgment. One of the most influential preachers of the late middle ages, he once called himself the Angel of Judgment (cf. Apocalypse 14:16).[167] In a striking anticipation of the doctrine of Vassula (see chapter 2 above), he taught that after the Antichrist there would come a perfect age of the Church, in which all mankind will return to belief in Christ.[168] One of his works, speaks of two antichrists, one '*mixtus*', and one '*purus*'. Between the two the Church would be

St. Vincent

renewed under a true pope and in a return to apostolic poverty.[169]

---

[164] Reeves, p. 338. On the latter point, Reeves accepts the opinion of Jorgensen, while remarking that it is difficult to find precise proof for it in the *Revelations*.

[165] Ibid.

[166] See p. xxx.

[167] *Butler's Lives of the Saints*, edited by D. Thurston and LD. Attwater (New York, Kennedy, 1956), vol. 2, p. 33.

[168] Vincent Ferrer, "Sermo de Sancto Dominico," *Sermones de Sanctis* (Antwerp, 1573), p. 299 (Reeves p. 171 n. 2).

[169] Vincent Ferrer, *Mirabile Opusculum de Fine Mundi* (1483, without any place of publication; Reeves ibid.)

Blessed Amadeus

Much later, a Portuguese Franciscan, Joannes Menesius de Sylva, later known as Blessed Amadeus, was invited to Rome by Pope Sixtus IV (1471-1484). There he founded a Franciscan community of strict observance, which later became absorbed into the Observantine branch of the Order. A man much venerated, he composed an *Apocalipsis Nova* which, according to legend, was dictated to him by the angel Gabriel. Focussing particularly on the Angelic Pope, it became quite popular, but by the same token suffered many interpolations, some of which provoked heated criticism of the author.[170]

Joachim of Fiore

Probably the most influential of prophetic voices during this period, and often the unspoken background of the others, was the

Joachim of Fiore
Woodcut from the *Commentary on Jeremiah,* Venice 1516

Calabrian abbot Joachim of Fiore (c. 1135-1202). He is well known for the idea that the Old Testament corresponded to the Age of the Father and the New Testament the Age of the Son, whereas soon to come was the Age of the Holy Spirit. The first was the age of married couples and the second that of the clergy, while the third would be characterized especially by contemplative monks - spiritual men. Joachim believed that the Antichrist had already been born, and thought it probable that he himself might live to see him. He is also reported as having predicted that Pope Innocent III would not have a successor. And close to the end of the twelfth century, "he was awaiting the year 1200 and what would follow it" with "concentrated attention."[171]

---

[170] Reeves 233-4, 440-441.

[171] Reeves, pp. 13, 14.

Although some of Joachim's positions had been condemned by the Fourth Lateran Council in 1215 and by Pope Alexander IV in 1256, his prophetic views continued to ferment in various nooks and corners of Christian thought for centuries. The Italian Augustinians took a great interest in him towards the end of the fifteenth century, and the first printed editions of his writings (by Meuccio) were brought out with the encouragement of their superior general, Cardinal Egidio.[172]

Moreover, his great fame inspired many writings published under his pseudonym. One of the more important was the *Oraculum Cyrilli*,[173] which purported to have been communicated by an angel to a Carmelite named Cyril, and transmitted by him to Joachim. Today, however, it is considered to be the work of the Spiritual Franciscans around 1280-1290.[174] Such Pseudo-Joachimist prophecies flourished in the fourteenth century.[175]

Rupescissa

In 1322, a Frenchman, Jean de Roquetaillade (alias Rupescissa), upon entering the Order of Friars Minor, claimed to have had a vision concerning the Antichrist, the first of many visions that marked his life. Ardently devoted to the ideal of absolute poverty, he aroused much opposition in the Order, and was eventually put into a Franciscan prison, where most of his writing was done. He greatly admired Joachim, although the works he was acquainted with were mostly spurious. He believed that after great tribulations the world would attain the millennium, in which the Church would be reformed by a Franciscan Pope. There would be several Antichrists, the final one a Hohenstaufen emperor, who would be overcome by the King of France, who in turn would support the Angelic Pope.[176]

---

[172] Reeves, Part I and Passim.
[173] An excerpt of this work is translated by McGinn, p. 192f.
[174] Reeves, p. 57.
[175] Reeves, p. 92.
[176] Reeves, pp. 226-227, 321-324.

Compilations

Compilations of such apocalyptic prophecies began to be drawn up during the fourteenth century. An English Augustinian, John of Erghome, produced a *Compilationes Vaticiniorum* drawn from the writings of Methodius, Joachim, Cyril the Carmelite, John Bridlington, Robert Userius, Roquetaillade, John Barsignacius, the Sibyl and others.[177]

A more important compilation was put together somewhere in the period 1356-1390 by a Calabrian hermit who went by the pseudonym, *Telesphorus of Cosenza*. He claimed that a vision of angels directed him to search the oracles of Cyril, Joachim and others concerning the Schism (which began in 1378) and the future age of the Holy Spirit. Like others of his time, he regarded the Schism as the fulfillment and confirmation of their prophecies.[178] The collection of Telesphorus was widely circulated in manuscript from the fifteenth to the seventeenth centuries[179] and was printed by the Augustinian, Sylvester Meuccio in 1516, the very year the Lateran Council forbade preachers to use such material.

The work of Telesphorus was carried forward by a fifteenth-century Dominican in Venice, Rusticianus, who added material from St. Bridget, St. Vincent Ferrer and from a Fr. Antonius de Yspania. According to him, the *Antichristus mixtus* was near at hand. He would be a false Pope, of German nationality, installed fraudulently and forcibly by the emperor. He in turn would crown a false German emperor (the expected Frederick III). Acting in concert, the two of the "would overturn France, devastate Italy, persecute the clergy, and profane St. Peter's." Altogether there would be three false popes; but they in turn would be overthrown by a combination of the Angelic Pope and the French king, who would bring about the Age of Tranquility.[180]

---

[177] Reeves, pp. 254-6. Erghome's work has been lost, but its contents have been summarized by Augustinian bibliographers. Erghome also composed a still-extant commentary on the prophecies of Bridlington.

[178] *Libellus Fratris Theolosphori de Cusentia...* (Venice, 1516), f. 9r. Reeves, p. 325, 423.

[179] Reeves, p. 327.

[180] Reeves, pp. 173, 343.

Other compilations of prophecies were published in 1454 (by Domenico Mauroceno),[181] in 1455 (by Jean du Bois),[182] in 1474 the *Tractatus de Turcis* (by some Dominicans),[183] in 1476 (anonymous), in 1488 (by Lichtenberger).[184] An important French compilation, *Mirabilis liber*,[185] came out in 1516, the year of the conciliar decree we are considering. Many more continued to appear in the years following the Council. The richest such collection was compiled by a Protestant, Johann Wolf, in 1600.[186]

Theologians

Interest in these prophetic writings was by no means confined to a circle of eccentrics. Some of the most prominent and intelligent men of the times took them very seriously. Pierre d'Ailly (1350-1420), chancellor of the University of Paris, Bishop of Cambrai, and finally Cardinal, asked whether the Great Schism might not be "that great schism which is supposed to be a preamble to the coming of Antichrist, and about which St. Hildegard and the venerable Abbot Joachim have written much."[187]

His student and successor as chancellor in Paris, Jean Gerson (1363-1429), is famous as one of the first theologians to look favorably on the visions of Joan of Arc.[188] He composed two classic works on discernment: *On Distinguishing True Visions From False*[189] in 1401, and *On the Testing of Spirits*[190] in 1415. In the latter, he manifested his disdain for the revelations of St. Bridget,[191] as he did for those of St. Catherine of Siena in a later work concerned with false prophecies.[192]

---

[181] Reeves, p. 343.

[182] Reeves, p. 42.

[183] Reeves, p. 325.

[184] Reeves, p. 347.

[185] Reeves, pp. 379-80.

[186] Reeves, pp. 487-88.

[187] Petrus de Aliaco, *Concordantia Astronomie cum Theologia...* (Venice, 1490, unpag.). Reeves, p. 422.

[188] See chapter 3 above [pp. 5-6].

[189] J. Gerson, *De Distinctione Verarum Visionum a Falsis, Oeuvres Complètes* ed. Glorieux (Paris, Desclée, 1960 ff.) vol. III, pp. 36-56.

[190] Jean Gerson, *De Probatione Spirituum*, Glorieux ed. vol. IX, pp. 177-185.

[191] Jean Gerson, *De Probatione Spirituum*, Glorieux ed. p. 179.

[192] J. Gerson, *De Examinatione Doctrinarum*. Glorieux ed. vol. IX, p. 469.

Henry of Langenstein (1325-1397), professor of theology at Paris and later Vice-Chancellor of the University of Vienna, was fascinated by predictions of the Last Things, particularly those dealing with the Antichrist. In a sermon before the whole University of Vienna, he publicly expressed his confidence in private revelations and in the methods of Joachim of Fiore. However, two years later, he reversed his position, denouncing Joachim, as well as Telesphorus of Cosenza and all recent prophets.[193] Cardinal Nicholas of Cusa (c. 1460-1464), a leader of the reform movement and participant at the Council of Basel, was convinced that the world would not last more than 300 years longer (i.e. not past 1734).[194]

Finally, the Fifth Lateran Council itself opened with an address that emphasized the coming chastisement and emendation of the Church.[195] The speaker was Cardinal Egidio of Viterbo, General of the Augustinian Order and also a leading reformer. Whether the conciliar decree with which we are concerned was conceived as a reprimand to him, I do not know. What is certain is that Edigio once asked one of his friars, Meuccio, to furnish him with the texts of Joachim of Fiore; and he encouraged Meuccio to publish the prophecies of Joachim during the period immediately following the Council (1516-1523).[196]

Summary

In summary, the Fifth Lateran Council convened in an age that was disturbed by apocalyptic prophecies about the coming purification of the Church and the proximate end of the world. These prophecies, nourished largely by the various reform movements then stirring in the Church, popularized the three figures of the World Emperor, the Angelic Pastor and the Antichrist. The chief source of the prophecies was Joachim of Fiore; but there were contributions

---

[193] *Tractatus Contra Quendam Eremitam de Ultimis Temporibus Vaticinantem Nomine Theolosphorum* (ed. B. Peza, *Thesaurus Anecdotorum Novissimus*, Augsburg, 1721); Reeves, p. 426.

[194] Ronald Knox, *Enthusiasm* (Oxford University Press, 1950), p. 137 (relying on the article "Cusanus," in the *Encyclopedia Britannia*).

[195] Reeves, 267 ff.

[196] Reeves, 267 ff.

also from more credible figures such as St. Bridget of Sweden and St. Vincent Ferrer. All of their writings, however, tended to be corrupted and interpolated as they got into popular circulation, especially through compilations that were made during the fourteenth, fifteenth and sixteenth centuries. It was the inordinate use of such prophecies and associated 'revelations' by preachers that the Council sought to curb.

Lateran V and the CDF

What light does Lateran V shed on the 1978 decree by the Congregation for the Doctrine of the Faith? In the first place, some contrasts between them should be noted. Lateran V was mainly concerned with prophecies, whereas the CDF is dealing specifically with apparitions (the latter do not seem to have been an important issue in the sixteenth century). In between, the 1917 Code of Canon Law treated prophecies and apparitions together, appropriately enough, since the principles for dealing with them both seem to be largely the same.

Secondly, Lateran V was concerned specifically with the use made of such prophecies by preachers, whereas the regulations of the CDF have to do more with cult and manifestations of devotion; it does not speak of preaching at all.

We noted above that Lateran V by no means rules out the possibility of authentic prophetic messages; on the contrary, it seems to expect that they will occur. However, it reserves judgment of such matters to the Holy See. Only when the affair is urgent is it to be dealt with by the local bishop. The CDF, on the contrary, makes the bishop the normal judge in the first instance. This is, of course, in accord with the tendency towards subsidiarity characteristic of our times in contrast with the more centralized procedure of the sixteenth century.

The Lateran Council did not discuss the criteria for discernment (even though Jean Gerson had already composed his great treatises a century earlier). The CDF, on the contrary, gives at least a rudimentary set of criteria.

The notions of the Last Great Emperor and the Angelic Pope, so prominent in fifteenth century prophecy, have been almost completely forgotten today.[197] Likewise, the coming of Antichrist, which was central to fifteenth century prophecy, is little mentioned in modern apparitions (important exceptions being Vassula and Father Gobbi - chapter 2 above).

On the other hand, two of the main themes of the modern apparitions are like echoes of the fifteenth century. The messages from both the fifteenth and twentieth centuries warn about a severe chastisement that is to come soon because of the prevailing sinfulness. Both likewise offer the reassurance that, after being purified, the Church as well as the world will enjoy a period of blessedness surpassing any hitherto known.

For me, this last was the most surprising result of this investigation, and I don't know yet what to make of it. Could these themes represent nothing more than perennial yearnings of Christians concerned for the renewal of Church and society? Or do they belong to a message enunciated by the authentic prophets of the fifteenth century (though often distorted by pseudo-prophets), and now being expressed again by the visionaries of our own time? Only a very painstaking study could determine which, if either, of these theses is correct.

---

[197] However, while composing this study, I encountered a recent but undated pamphlet by Stephen C. Mahowald, *The Great Chastisement. An Introduction* (MMR Publishing, POB 37358, Omaha, Nebraska 68137), containing a brief chapter on "The great monarch and the holy pope." To the so-called prophecies of St. Methodius, St. Cataldus and other staples of the fifteenth century compilations, he adds more from the seventeenth, eighteenth and nineteenth centuries.

WHY ALL THESE MARIAN APPARITIONS TODAY

BIBLIOGRAPHY
The theology of apparitions[1]

1401 Gerson, Jean, *De Distinctione Verarum Visionum a Falsis. Oeuvres Complètes*, ed. Glorieux, vol. III, 90 (1961). An English translation is available in *The Concept of Discretio Spirituum in John Gerson's "De Probatione Spirituum" and "De Distinctione Verarum Visionum a Falsis"* by Paschal Boland O.S.B. (Catholic University of America Press, Washington D.C., 1959). In chapter 3, however, I have used my own translations.

1415 Gerson, Jean, *De Probatione Spirituum*, ibid. vol. XI, #448. English translation as in the preceding entry.

1423 Gerson, Jean, *De Examinatione Doctrinarum*, ibid. vol. IX, #456.

1429 Gerson, Jean, *De Puella Aurelianensi*, ibid. vol. IX, #476.

1445-46 Turrecremata, Joannes de, *Declarationes Revelationum S. Birgittae, cum Epistola pro Eisdem Apologetica*, Basel. (The first five chapters are often published in editions of the works of St. Brigid; the remaining chapters [6-123] have been reprinted in Mansi, *Sacrorum Conciliorum Nova et Amplissima Collectio...*, Florence, Venice, Paris and Leipzig, 1759-1927, vol. XXX, 699-814).

1593-1603 del Rio, Martinus, *Disquisitionum Magicarum Libri Sex*. Mainz.

1600 Thyraeus, *De Apparitionibus Spirituum*, Cologne. (Reprinted in 1605).

1617 Suarez, Francisco de, S.J. *De Angelis*, IV, c. 23, n. 5 (*Opera Omnia* II, Paris Vivès, 1856, p. 537).

1623 Binsfield, Pierre, *De Confessionibus Maleficorum et Sagarum*, Köln.

1638 Gravina, Domenico, O.P. *Ad Discernendas Veras a Falsis Revelationibus: Basanites, Hoc est Lapis Lydius, Theoricam et Praxim Complectens*, Neapoli, typis S. Bonini.

---

[1] This bibliography has been arranged in chronological order in order to illustrate the historical development of the doctrine. As a rule, only works dealing with the *theology* of apparitions are included here, as well as the chronological reports by Sausseret (1854) and Ernst (1983, 1989). Accounts of particular apparitions are not included (although many are noted in chapter I). Likewise, treatises on spiritual and mystical theology, which usually devote a few pages to this subject, have not been included. For a report on the more important of them, see the 1993 article by Adnès.

1734-1738 Lambertini, P. (later Pope Benedict XIV), *Doctrina de Servorum Dei Beatificatione et de Beatorum Canonizatione....* 4 vols. Republished at Prato, 1839-1840. This work was written by the Cardinal before he became Pope. Even though he republished it as Benedict XIV, he declared plainly in the preface that this was a work of merely human authority, not an act of papal magisterium. Cardinal de Azevedo published a "Synopsis" of the work in 1749 (Rome, Salomon, 1749). For our subject note: Lib. II, c. 32, "De adnotatis et adnotandis per revisores super visionibus, revelationibus et prophetiis"; lib. III, c. 50-53: "De visionibus et apparitionibus... De revelationibus"; lib. IV, pars I, c. 32: "De beatorum, et sanctorum apparitionibus, an inter miracula recenseri possint."

1744 Amort, E., *De Revelationibus et Apparitionibus Privatis. Regulae tutae ex Scriptura, Conciliis, SS. Patribus, Aliisque Optimis Authoribus Collectae, Explicatae et Exemplis Illustratae*, Augustae Vindelicorum, M. Veith. (Against the visions of Maria of Agreda.)

1746 Calmet, Auguste. *Dissertations sur les Apparitions des Anges, des Démons et des Esprits, et sur les Revenants et les Vampires*, Paris.

1749 Amort, E., *Controversia de Revelationibus Agredeanis Explicatae cum Epicrisi ad Ineptas Earum Revelationum Vindicias*, editas a P. Didaco Gonzales Mattheo et P. Landelino Mayr, Augustae Vindelicorum et Herbipoli, J. Veith.

1751 Lenglet de Fresnoy, Nicolas, *Traité Historique et Dogmatique sur les Apparitions, les Visions et les Révélations Particulières*, Avignon/Paris, Leloup. (Includes the 1746 treatise by Dom Calmet.)

1836-1842 Görres, Joseph von, *Die Christliche Mystik* (Regensburg) II, 307-380.

1854 Sausseret, Paul, *Apparitions et Révélations de la Trés Sainte Vierge depuis l'Origine du Christianisme jusqu'à nos Jours*, 2 vol. Paris, Vives.

1899 Knauer, E. *Die Vision im Lichte der Kulturgeschichte.*

1901 Forget, J. "Apparition," in *Dictionnaire de Théologie Catholique*, 1/2.

1908 Saudreau, A. *Les Faits Extraordinaires de la Vie Spirituelle*, Paris, pp. 80-86, 225-231.

1913 Didiot, J. "Apparitions," *Dictionnaire Apologétique de la Foi Catholique*, Paris, Beauchesne, vol. I, col. 283-285.

1923 Farges, A. *Les Phénomènes Mystiques Distingués de Leurs Contrefaçons Humaines et Diaboliques*, 2nd. ed. Paris, Pp. 7-34.

1924 Voigt, M. *Beiträge zur Geschichte der Visionen-Literatur im Mittelalter.*

1925 Roure, Lucien, "Apparitions et Visions" in *Dictionnaire Pratique des Donnaissances Religieuses*, Paris, Letouzey, I, 343-347.

1928 Didiot, J. "Révélations Privées," in *Dictionnaire Apologétique de la Foi Catholique*, Paris, Beauchesne, vol. IV, col. 1008-1009.

1929 Bergier, Abbé, "Apparitions" in *Dictionnaire de Théologie*, I, Paris. (Devoted almost exclusively to biblical apparitions).

1934 Tonquédec, J. de, "Apparitions" in *Dictionnaire de Spiritualité*, I, col. 802-809.

1937 Congar, Yves, "La Crédibilité des Révélationes Privées," *Vie Spirituelle. Supplément* 53, 29-48.

1937 Forget, J. "Apparitions," *Dictionnaire Apologétique de la Foi Catholique* Letouzey et Ané, t. I/2 col. 1687-1692.

1941 Gabriele de Santa Maria Maddalene, O.C.D. *Visioni e Rivelazioni Nella Vita Spirituale*, Firenze. (ET *Visions and Revelations in the Spiritual Life*. Westminster MD, Newman, 1950)

1941 Lais, H. *Eusebius Amort und Seine Lehre Über die Privatoffenbarungen*, Freiburg i. Br.

1948 Carpino, Francesco, "Apparizione," in *Enciclopedia Cattolica*, I, Città del Vaticano, II Libro Cattolico, 1700-1702.

1948 Colombo, Carlo, "Apparizioni et Messagi Divini Nella Vita Cristiana," *La Scuola Cattolica* 76, pp. 265-278.

1948 Oddone, A. "Visioni et apparizione," in *Civiltà Cattolica* 99, I, 359-370; II 364-375.

1948 Rotureau, G. "Apparitions et Visions," in *Catholicisme*, Paris, Letouzey, I.

1949 Rahner, Karl, S.J., "Notions Théologiques sur les Révélations Privées," *Revue d'Ascétique et Mystique* 25, pp. 506-514.

1949 Staehlin, J.M., "Apariciones," *Razon y Fe* 139, pp. 443-464; 546-562; 140, pp. 71-98.

1950 Ranwez, E., "Révélations Privées," *Revue Diocésaine de Namur*, Juillet 5, pp. 165-178; 318-333.

1950 Zühringer, D. "Muttergottes Erscheinungen," *Benediktinische Monatschrift* 26, 25-40.

1950 [Anonymous] "Aparicion," *Enciclopedia de la Religion Catolica*, Barcelona, I, 781-782.

1951 Ottaviani, "Siate, Cristiani, a Muoveri Piu Gravi," *Osservatore Romano*, Febr. 4, 1951, pp. 11-2. (French translation in *Documentation Catholique*, 48 [1951], 25 mars, col. 3514-356.)

1952 Goubert, J. and Cristiani, L. *Les Apparitions de la Sainte Vierge.* Ed. de la Colombe.

1952 Lhermitte, J. *Mystiques et Faux Mystiques*, Paris, Bloud et Gay.

1954 Castellano, Mario, "La Prassi Canonica Circa le Apparizioni Mariane," *Enciclopedia Mariana, "Theotokos"*, Gênes, Bevilacqua & Solari; Milano, Editrice Massimo. (3rd ed. 1958)

1954 Lochet, Louis, "Apparitions," *Nouvelle Revue Théologique* 76, pp. 949-464.

1956 Réginald-Omet, R. P. *Supranormal ou Surnaturel?*, Paris, Fayard.

1956 *Virgo Immaculata*, vol. 16, *De Apparitionibus Virginis Immaculatae*, Roma, Academia Mariana. Note especially:

Truhlar, Carolus, S.J., "Principia Theologica de Habitudine Christiani erga Apparitiones," pp. 1-17.

1957 Baliç, Carlo, "Apparizioni Mariane dei Secoli XIX-XX" in *Enciclopedia Mariana "Theotokos,"* 2nd ed. Genoa & Milan, pp. 245-254. (1st ed. 1954)

1957 Lochet, Louis, *Apparitions*, Paris, Desclée de Brouwer.

1957 Maréchal, H.-L. *Mémorial des Apparitions de la Vierge dans l'Eglise.* Paris, Cerf.

1958 Baliç, Carlo, "De Auctoritate Ecclesiae circa Apparitiones seu Revelationes," *Divinitas* 2, pp. 85-103.

1958 Holstein, H., "Les Apparitions Mariales," in *Maria. Etudes sur la Sainte Vierge*, edited by Hubert du Manoir, Paris, Beauchesne, tome V, pp. 757-778.

1958 Laurentin, R. *Lourdes. Documents Authentiques* Paris, Lethielleux. Chapter 2, 3, pp. 99-108 (On the Function and Limit of Apparitions).

1958 Laurentin, René, *Multiplication des Apparitions de la Vierge Aujourd'hui* Paris, Fayard.

1958 Rahner, Karl, *Visionen und Prophezeiungen* Innsbruck, Herder. (ET *Visions and Prophecies*, London, Burns and Oates, 1963).

Review by L. Volken, "Um die Theologische Bedeutung der Privatoffenbarungen," *Freiburger Zeitschrift für Philosophie und Theologie*, 6 (1959), pp. 431-439.

1960 Branz, F. *"Ich komme vom Himmel" Prophetie auch heute*?

1961 Herran, Laurentino M. "Historia, Myto et Leyenda en las Apariciones de la Virgen," *Estudios Marianos*, XXII, pp. 243-272.

1961 Volken, Laurent, *Les Révélations dans l'Eglise*. Mulhouse, Salvator. (ET *Visions, Revelations and the Church*, New York, Kenedy, 1963.)

1961 *Cahiers Marials*, Janvier-février, n. 25, "Les Apparitions Mariales dans la Vie de l'Eglise" (articles by Cazelles, Michel and Laurentin).

1962 Ahlenstiel, H. *Vision und Traum*, Stuttgart.

1962 *Apparitiones Marianae Earumque Momentum in Ecclesia*. (*Maria et Ecclesia*, vol. XII). Rome, Pontificia Academia Mariana Internationalis. (Proceedings of the International Mariological Congress held at Lourdes in 1958). Note in particular:

Valentini, Eugenio, S.D., "Rivelazioni Private et Fatti Dommatici," pp. 1-9.

Roy, Dom François, O.S.B., "Le Fait de Lourdes Devant le Magistère," pp. 11-56.

Zavalloni, P. Robertus, O.F.M., "De Apparitionum Phaenomeno-Logia," pp. 307-335.

1964 Benz, Ernst. "Vision and Führung in der Christlichen Mystik," in *Eranos-Jahrbuch XXX*.

1964 Laurentin, René. "Bulletin Marial," *Revue des Sciences Philosophiques et Théologiques* 48, pp. 116-119 (review of the 1962 articles by Valentini and Roy).

1966 Iturioza, D.J., *Revelaciones Privadas, Estudio Teologico*, Madrid.

1967 Aumann, Jordan, "Visions...," *New Catholic Encyclopedia*, New York, McGraw-Hill, vol. XIV, col. 716-717.

1967 Manteau-Bonamy, H.-M. O.P., "Les Apparitions Mariales à la Lumière de la Théologie des Charismes et de la Vertu d'Espérance," *Le Rosaire dans la Pastorale*, Octobre 1967, n. 12, pp. 15-18.

1967 Manteau-Bonamy, H.-M. O.P., "Congrès de Lisbonne-Fatima," in *Cahiers Marials*, 15 novembre 1967, n. 60, pp. 310-314 (On the Conclusions of the Congress about Apparitions).

1967 Sanchez-Ventura, F. *Stigmatisés et Apparitions*, N.E.L.

1968 Billet, B. "Apparitions et Sanctuaires," *Cahiers Marials*, 1 septembre, n. 64, pp. 233-238.

1968 Laurentin, R. "Bulletin sur la Vierge Marie," *Revue des Sciences Philosophiques et Théologiques* 52, pp. 529-530 (On the Function and Status of Apparitions).

1968 Lochet, Louis, *Apparitions. Presence de Marie à Notre Temps*, 3rd ed. Paris, Desclée de Brouwer. (ET *Apparitions of Our Lady. Their Place in the life of the Church*, New York, Herder and Herder, 1960.)

1969 Billet, B. "Le Problème Pastoral des Fausses Apparitions dans l'Histoire de Notre Temps," *Le Rosaire dans la Pastoral*, N. 19, juillet, pp. 33-38.

1969 Benz, E. *Die Vision, Ehrfarungsformen und Bilderwelt*, Stuttgart, Klet.

1970 *De Primordiis Cultus Mariani*, (Proceedings of the Mariological Congress of Lisbon and Fatima), vol. VI, Roma, Academia Mariana. Note especially:

Enrique del Sagrado Corazon, O.C.D. "Las Apariciones Marianas en el Ambiente Ecuménico," pp. 13-52.

Manteau-Bonamy, H.-M., O.P., "Les Interventions de Marie et l'Espérance de l'Eglise," pp. 417-422.

Moreira-Ferraz, Agosthino, S.J., "A Teologia das Revelçoes Privadas Francisco Suarez e a sua Possivel Incidencia Sobre Fatima," pp. 207-222.

Ortiz de Urbina, I., S.J., "La Actitude de la Iglesia ante las Apariciones de la Virgen," pp. 3-12.

1970 Laurentin, R. "Bulletin sur la Vierge Marie," *Revue des Sciences Philosophiques et Théologiques* 54, pp. 308-313 (On the Function of Apparitions).

1971 B. Billet and others, *Vraies et Fausses Apparitions dans l'Eglise*, Paris. 2nd ed. 1976 Lethielleux (Proceedings of a Conference of the French Mariological Society). In particular, note:

Billet, Bernard, O.S.B. "Le Fait des Apparitions non Reconnues par l'Eglise," pp. 7-58.

Laurentin, R., "Fonction et Statut des Apparitions," pp. 153-205.

Oraison, Marc, "Le Point de Vue du Médecin Psychiatre Clinicien sur les Apparitions," pp. 127-151.

1975 Macca, V. and M. Caprioli, "Comunicazioni Mistiche," in *Dizionario Enciclopedico di Spiritualità*, Rome, Citta Nuova Editrice, I.

1976/77 Guillaumont, A. "Les Visions Mystiques dans le Monachisme Oriental Chrètien," *Colloque sur les Visions Mystiques*, in *Nouvelles de l'Institut Catholique de Paris*, 124-127.

1977 Tizane, Emile. *Les Apparitions de la Vierge: un Enquêteur s'Interroge*, Tchou.

1977 Turchini-Zuccarelli, C. *Les Merveilleuses Apparitions de Notre-Dame*, N.E.L.

1978 Sola, Francisco de P. "Problematica Teologica de las Apariciones Marianas. Criterios de la Jerarquia," *Espiritu*, vol. XXVII, n. 77, pp. 9-45.

1979 Labourdette, M.-M. "Sainte Bernadette et le Problème des Apparitions," *Revue Thomiste* 79, pp. 483-499.

1979 Schallenberg, G. *Visionäre Erlebnisse im 20. Jahrhundert. Eine Psychopathologische Untersuchung*.

1981 Dinzelbacher, P. *Vision und Visionsliteratur im Mittelalter*, Stuttgart, Hiersemann.

1982 Scheffczyk, L. *Die Theologischen Grundlagen von Erscheinungen und Prophezeiungen*.

1983 Carroll, Michael P. "Visions of the Virgin Mary," *Journal for the Scientific Study of Religion*, 22, pp. 205-221.

1983 Ernst, R. *Maria Redet zu Uns. Marien-Erscheinungen Seit 1830*.

1983 Jaffe, Aniella, *Apparitions. Fantômes, Rêves et Mythes*, Mercure de France-Lemail.

1983 Laurentin, René. "Apparitions," in *Les Routes de Dieu. Aux Sources de la Religion Populaire*, Paris, O.E.I.L., pp. 91-135.

1983 Laurentin, René, *Pélerinages, Sanctuaires, Apparitions*, Paris, O.E.I.L.

1984 Ancilli, E. "Le Visioni et le Rivelazioni," in *La Mistica. Fenemenologia e Riflessione Teologica*, II, 1984, pp. 473-481.

1984 Laurentin, René, "Marienerscheinungen" in *Handbuch der Marienkunde* ed. Wolfgang Beinert & H. Petri, Regensburg, Pustet, pp. 528-555.

1984 Lawler, Ronald D. "Divine Faith, Private Revelation, Popular Devotion," *Marian Studies*, vol. XXXV, pp. 100-110.

1984 Schumacher, J. "Privatoffenbarungen und Marienverehrung," in *Marien-Erscheinungen und Gnadenbilder als Zeichen der Gotteskraft* ed. by G. Rovira, 66-132.

1985 Amat, J. *Songes et Visions. L'Au-Delà dans la Litterature Latine tardive*, Paris.

1985 Galot, Jean, "Les Apparitions dans la Vie de l'Eglise," *Esprit et Vie. L'Ami du Clergé*, no. 47, Nov. 21, pp. 609-615.

1985 Gazeau, Roger, "Les Apparitions," *Lettre de Ligugé*, 229, pp. 23-34.

1987 Adnès, Pierre. "Révélations priveés," in *Dictionnaire de Spiritualité*, XIII.

1987 Billet, B. "Apparitions Mariales," in *L'état des Religions dans le Monde*, Paris, La découverte-Cerf.

1987 Kammerer, Th. "Les Apparitions et les Visions au Regard de la Psychiatrie et de la Psychologie Religieuse," *Bulletin de l'Assocaiation médicale Internationale de Lourdes*, n. 217-218, avril.

1987 Vauchez, A. "Jeanne d'Arc et le Prophétisme Féminin des 14e et 14e siecles," c. 27 of *Les Laics au Moyen Age*, Paris.

1988 Besutti, Giuseppe M. *Facciamo il Punto Sulle Apparizioni Mariane*, Editrice Elle di Ci, Leumann.

1988 Laurentin, René. *Multiplication des Apparitions de la Vierge Aujourd'hui*. Fayard. (3rd ed. 1991)

1988 Pannet, Robert. *Les Apparitions Aujourd'hui*, Chambray (France), C.L.D.

1988 Turi, Anna Maria. *Pourquoi la Vierge Apparait Aujourd'hui?* Editions du Félin.

1989 Ernst, R. *Lexikon der Marien-Erscheinungen*, Altötting, Ruhland.

1989 Lais, H. "Erscheinungen," in *Marienlexikon*, ed. R. Bäumer and L. Scheffczyk. St. Ottilien: EOS Verlag, Bd. II.

1989 Laurentin, René, *The Church and Apparitions - Their Status and Function: Criteria and Reception* (Report at the National Conference on Medjugorje, University of Notre Dame, May 1989) Milford, OH, Riehle.

1989 Mucci, G. "Le Apparizione: Teologia e Discernimento," in *La Civiltà Cattolica*, 1989, 424-433.

1990 Laurentin, René, *Report on Apparitions*. Milford, OH, 45150, The Riehle Foundation, P.O.B. 7 (Note specially Part II, "True and False Apparitions: Contemporary Phenomenon.")

1990 Mucci, G. "Le Apparizioni, Allucinationi et Mistica," in *La Civiltà Cattolica*, 1990, 119-127.

1991 Dinzelbacher, Peter, *"Revelationes." Typologie des Sources du Moyen-éage Occidental*, Turnhout, Brepolis.

1991 Vergote, A. "Visions et Apparitions," in *Revue Théologique de Louvain*, 22 205-225.

1992 Barnay, Sylvie, "Les Apparitions de la Vierge," Paris, Cerf.

1993 Groeschel, Benedict, *A Still Small Voice*. San Francisco, Ignatius.

1993 Adnès, Pierre, "Visions," in *Dictionnaire de Spiritualité*, Paris, Beauchesne, 16, 949-1002.

1993 Freze, *Michael, Voices, Visions and Apparitions*. Huntington, IN, Our Sunday Visitor. (Not a very critical work, but it contains much useful information.)

1995 Chiron, Yves. *Enquête sur les Apparitions de la Vierge*, Perrin/Mame.